Birmingham Repertory Theatre Company with Hampstead Theatre
and Theatre Royal Plymouth presents

TENDER

by **Abi Morgan**

First performed at Hampstead Theatre on 6 September 2001

THE ATTACHMENT SCHEME

Two of the new plays in our Autumn season, *Tender* by Abi Morgan and *Behsharam* by Gurpreet Bhatti, began life as ideas on our attachment scheme for writers. This scheme was established in 1996 to nurture new plays for Birmingham Repertory Theatre, principally from first-time playwrights. Since then it has developed the work of over 20 playwrights with an increasing emphasis on supporting the work of local writers. The scheme provides them with the chance to research and explore their idea and, if appropriate, work with other professional playwrights, directors, designers, choreographers, actors and other practitioners to maximise its potential. The ultimate aim of the scheme is to provide work for the company to stage. The majority of attached plays go on to be commissioned by the theatre and the majority of these plays go on to receive full productions by the company.

The scheme is financially supported by Channel 4 Television.

Ray Grewal's *My Dad's Corner Shop*

Jess Walter's *Terracotta*

For further information about the scheme please contact:

Ben Payne or Caroline Jester
Literary Department
Birmingham Repertory Theatre
Broad Street
Birmingham B1 2EP
Telephone: 0121 245 2000

TENDER
by **Abi Morgan**

Squeal Nick Bagnall
Hen Caroline Faber
Tash Kate Fleetwood
Al David Kennedy
Nathan Sean O'Callaghan
Gloria Nicola Redmond
Marvin Benny Young

Director Anthony Clark
Designer Niki Turner
Sound Designer Gregory Clarke
Lighting Designer Vince Herbert
Assistant Director Pip Minnithorpe

Deputy Stage Manager Maggie Tully
Assistant Stage Manager Richard Llewelyn

Set built and painted by Birmingham Repertory Theatre

CAST

Nick Bagnall
Squeal

Training: Guildhall School of Music and Drama.
Theatre: *Henry VI: III* (RSC – World Tour); *The Machine Wreckers* (National Theatre); *Caravan* (Bush); *Hushabye Mountain* (Hampstead and Tour); *Meat* (Plymouth Theatre Royal); *Hamlet* (BOV); *Mr Heracles* (West Yorkshire Playhouse); *The Arbor, Voices on the Wind, Exit* (RNT Studio); *Hummingbird* (Old Red Lion); *The Changeling* (RNT Studio); *Erpingham Camp* (Assembly, Liverpool Everyman).
Television: *The Bill; Insiders; Silent Witness; Dalziel and Pascoe; The Gift; Nature Boy; Out of the Blue*.
Film: *Hysteria: The Def Leppard Story* (VHI and Viacom).
Radio: *A Midsummer Nights Dream, A Kestrel For a Knave* (Radio 3).

Caroline Faber
Hen

Training: Webber Douglas.
Theatre: Maggie 3 in *Mill On The Floss* for Shared Experience (New Ambassadors, London & World Tour); Maria in *The Heiress* (Royal National Theatre); Freda in *Dangerous Corner* (Watford Palace); Lady Nijo/ Win in *Top Girls* (Drum Theatre, Plymouth); Sarah in *The End of The Affair* (Salisbury Playhouse/ The Bridewell); Peta in *The Colonel Bird* (The Gate, Notting Hill); Edith in *Kind Hearts and Coronets* (Mercury, Colchester); The Witch in *Into The Woods* (Upstairs at the Landor); Fanny in *Cavalcade* (Sadlers Wells); Jessica in *The Merchant of Venice* (Salisbury Playhouse).
Television: *Midsomer Murders* (ITV); *Comedy Nation* (Channel 4); *Unnatural Acts* (Paramount); *Gamesmaster* (Channel 4).

Kate Fleetwood
Tash

Theatre: Chorus in *Medea* (Queen's Theatre); Gaoler's Daughter in *Two Noble Kinsmen*, Iris in *The Tempest* (The Globe); *Nativity,* Dinarzard/ Parizade in *Arabian Knights* (Young Vic); Regina in *Ghosts* (Theatre Royal Plymouth); Juliet in *Romeo and Juliet* (Greenwich and tour); Death/ Gabriel in *Comic Mysteries* (Oxford Stage Company); Nancy in *Swaggers* – Best Fringe play – Time Out Awards 1996 (Old Red Lion); Viola in *Twelfth Nigh*, Flaminia in *Love is the Drug* (Oxford Stage Company).

Television: Karen in *Eastenders*, Karina in *Holby City*, Alice in *Getting Hurt*, Eleanor in *Lizzie's Pictures* (BBC); Woman in *Urban Gothic: The End* (Channel 5); Maggie in *The Infinite Worlds of HG Wells* (Hallmark); *World's First*, Woman in *Catching Light* (Channel Four).

Film: Bora in *Beautiful People.*

David Kennedy
Al

Training: Webber Douglas Academy of Dramatic Art.

Theatre: Peter in *Meat* (Plymouth); Disciple in *Messiah* for Steven Berkoff (Edinburgh); Lee in *Hushabye Mountain* – Nominated for Best Actor Award – Manchester Evening News (Tour & Hampstead Theatre); Tyrrel/ Rivers in *Richard III*, Marco in *A View from the Bridge* (Leicester Haymarket); *Coriolanus* (Japan and Israel); Stanley in *Death of a Salesman* (Royal National Theatre); Frankie in *Dealer's Choice* (Vaudeville Theatre); Peter in *Blue Remembered Hills* (Cheltenham, Everyman); *The Hairy Ape* (Bristol Old Vic); Co.Sgt. Major in *Journey's End* (Village Theatre); Con in *All On Top* (Etcetera Theatre).

Television: *Undercover Cops; Without Motive; Big Smoke; Skin Deep; Trial and Retribution I & II; Love Bites: In Your Dreams; Dream Team; Supply and Demand; Strange But True; Nelson's Column; Moving Story; 99-1; All New Alexei Sayle Show; Soldier Soldier III; Pie In The Sky; Between the Lines; Frank Stubbs Promotes; The Bill.*

Film: *Reign of Fire* (due for release 2002); *Down; The Biographer; Shiner; Shooters; Billy Elliot; Gangster No. 1; Dreaming of Joseph Lees; Love is the Devil; Nil By Mouth; The Fifth Element; Mary Shelley's Frankenstein.*
Radio: *Central 822, Michael and Me* (BBC Radio 4).

Sean O'Callaghan
Nathan

Training: RADA.
Theatre: *Playboy of the Western World* (Liverpool Playhouse); *St Augustine's Oak* (The Globe); *Pentecost, After Easter, Son of Man, Henry V, Zenobia, A Brand For The Burning, Words, Words, Words, A Winter's Tale, Romeo & Juliet, Richard II, Country Dancing, The Storm, Class Enemy, Venus and Adonis* (RSC); *Uncle Vanya* (European Tour); *Ursula* (co-production with Birmingham Repertory Theatre), *Wounds to the Face, Ecstatic Bible* (Adelaide Festival) all with The Wrestling School; *A Bite of the Night* (Almeida); *Satan in Goray* (Tottering Bipeds); *Big Maggie, All My Sons, Soldiers Three, The Dirty Hill, Twelfth Night, The Bright and Bold Design, The Plough and the Stars, Overture, Julius Caesar, The Hunchback of Notre Dame* (New Vic Theatre).
Television: *Neverwhere; Supply and Demand; Lenny Henry; The Last Romantics; Medics; Casualty.*
Film: *Brand From the Burning; Father's Day; The Long Shot.*
Radio: *Knowledge and a Girl* (Radio 4).

Nicola Redmond
Gloria

Training: Central School of Speech and Drama.
For Birmingham Repertory Theatre: Dr Bright in *Perpetua.*
Theatre: Titania/ Hippolyta in *A Midsummer Night's Dream,* Beatrice in *Much Ado About Nothing* (Regent's Park); Mrs Tot in *The Tot Family* (Merlin Theatre, Budapest); Constance Wickstead in *Habeas Corpus* (International Tour); Austen/Mr Knightley in *Emma* (Gilded Balloon, Edinburgh); Maggie O'Brian in *With Love From Nicolai* (Bristol Old Vic/ Teatrul Dramatic, Romania); Sarah

McKenna in *Waking*, Julia in *Me and My Friend*, Jo Beth in *Children of the Dust* (Soho Theatre); Julia in *The Duchess of Malfi, Cheek by Jowl* (Wyndhams/ World Tour); Helen/ Emma in *Bearing Fruit* (Hampstead Theatre); Irene in *Rag Doll*, Ann in *Where's Willy* (Bristol Old Vic); Macu in *The Baby*, Renata in *Phoenix*, Pauline in *Shang-a-Lang* (Bush Theatre); Lady Macduff in *Macbeth*, Imogen Parrott in *Trelawney of the Wells*, Gypsy in *The Beaux Stratagem* (Royal National Theatre); Christine in *Body and Soul* (Albery Theatre); Masha in *The Three Sisters*, Portia in *The Merchant of Venice* (Wolsey, Ipswich); Jane Pilkings in *Death & The King's Horseman* (Royal Exchange); Pierette in *The Good Sisters* (Crucible, Sheffield); Doctor in *The Orphan's Comedy* (Traverse Theatre); Elizabeth I in *Vivat! Vivat Regina!* Ruth in *Blithe Spirit* (Pitlochry).
Television: *Anybody's Nightmare; Eastenders; The Cazalet Chronicles; Casualty; Gooseberries Don't Dance; The Phoenix & the Carpet; Silent Witness (II); Secret House of Death; Goodnight Sweetheart; In Suspicious Circumstances – The Case of Esther Pay; Pie in The Sky; Where's Willy; Rag Doll; Three, Seven, Eleven I & II; Me & My Friend; Family; Harry's Kingdom; Boy Soldier; Morphine & Dolly Mixtures; Capital Sins; Joan.*
Film: *Come Together.*

Benny Young
Marvin

Training: R.S.A.M.D.
Theatre: *Flight, Battle Royal, Albert Speer, Romeo and Juliet, Peer Gynt, Playboy of the Western World* (Royal National Theatre); *Richard III, Henry V, A General From America (Royal Shakespeare Company); The Iceman Cometh* (Old Vic); *Hosanna* (Tron Theatre); *Kong Lives, Walter, The Hardman, Kora, Walter, Anna Campbell* (Traverse); *Seven Lears, Folgo, Victory, The Europeans* (The Wrestling School).
Television: *The Kid in the Corner; King Lear; Coronation Street; Boon; The Bill; Taggart.*
Radio: *Weir of Hermision; Confessions of a Justified Sinner.*
Film: *Chariots of Fire; Out of Africa; Funny Man; Hostage; Girl in The Picture.*

Abi Morgan
Writer

Theatre: *Tiny Dynamite* (Paines Plough, Frantic Assembly 2001); *Splendour* (Paines Plough at Traverse Theatre, Edinburgh Festival 2000 and tour); *Fast Food* (Royal Exchange Theatre, Manchester, March 1999); *Moment is a Gift* (1999) and *Fortune* (2000), both for Paines Plough/ Prada; *Sleeping Around* (1997/8 commission from Paines Plough to write with three other writers: Mark Ravenhill, Hilary Fannin and Stephen Greenhorn. Produced 1998 at the Donmar Warehouse and on tour); *Skinned* (shortlisted for the Allied Domecq Award at the Bush Theatre. Toured by the Nuffield Theatre in 1998). Film/ television credits include: *My Fragile Heart* (Tiger Aspect/ ITV September 2000); *Peak Practice* (Carlton/ITV); *Murder* (currently filming, Oct 2001). Abi is also currently under commission to Royal Exchange, Manchester, RNT and Out of Joint.

Anthony Clark
Director

Anthony began his career at The Orange Tree Theatre, directing everything from a school's tour of *Macbeth* to Martin Crimp's first play *Living Remains.* In 1983, he joined Tara Arts to direct their first two professional productions, *Lion's Raj* and *Ancestral Voices.* A year later he was appointed Artistic Director of Contact Theatre in Manchester where his productions included, *Romeo and Juliet, Midsummer Night's Dream, The Duchess of Malfi, Blood Wedding* (Manchester Evening News Best Production Award), *Mother Courage and her Children, Oedipus, To Kill A Mockingbird* (Manchester Evening News Best Production Award), *The Power of Darkness* and new plays *Two Wheeled Tricycle* by John Chambers, *Face Value* by Cindy Artiste, *Green* by Tony Clark, *Homeland* by Ken Blakeson and *McAlpine's Fusiliers* by Kevin Fegan. He joined Birmingham Repertory Theatre Company in 1990 as Associate Director. His many productions for Birmingham include *Macbeth, Julius Caesar, Aetheist's Tragedy* (TMA Best Director Award), *The Seagull, Threepenny Opera, Saturday Sunday Monday, The Playboy of the Western World, Pygmalion, St Joan, The Entertainer* and David Lodge's *Home Truths.* In 1997 he was appointed Associate Artistic Director responsible for the launch and programme of The Door (formerly The Rep Studio), dedicated exclusively to the promotion of new work. His recent productions there include *Playing by The Rules* by Rod Dungate, *Nervous Women* by Sara Woods, *Rough* by Kate Dean, *Syme* (co-production with NT Studio) by Michael Bourdages, *True Brit* by Ken Blakeson, *Confidence* by Judy Upton, *Down Red Lane* by Kate Dean, *Paddy Irishmen* (co-production with the Tricycle Theatre) by Declan Croghan, *All That Trouble* by Paul Lucas, *Silence* (co-production with Theatre Royal Plymouth) by Moira Buffini, *My Best Friend* (co-production with Hampstead Theatre) by Tamsin Oglesby, *Slight Witch* (co-production with NT Studio) by Paul Lucas and *Belonging* by Kaite O'Reillly. He has freelanced extensively including *Dr Faustus* (The Young Vic), *The Red Balloon* (Bristol Old Vic and RNT – TMA Best Show for Young People Award), *The Snowman* (Leicester Haymarket), *Mother Courage and Her Children* (RNT), *The Day After Tomorrow* (RNT), *The Wood Demon* (Playhouse) and *Loveplay* (RSC) by Moira Buffini.

Niki Turner
Designer

Niki's design credits include: The 2001 National Opera Studio Showcase (Queen Elizabeth Hall); *Further Than The Furthest Thing* (Royal National Theatre/Tron Theatre/Traverse Theatre, Fringe First Award, Edinburgh Festival 2000); *Embryonic Dreams* (Edinburgh Festival 2001); *As You Like It* (co-design with Kaffe Fassett); *Oroonoko* (RSC); *Speaking In Tongues* (Hampstead Theatre/Derby Playhouse); *Danny Bouncing* (Derby Playhouse); *The Beatification of Area Boy* (West Yorkshire Playhouse and World Tour including Brooklyn Academy); *Things Fall Apart* (Royal Court/West Yorkshire Playhouse as part of LIFT and USA/UK Tour); *Junk* (Oxford Stage Company/Den Nationale Scene Norway); *Yerma* (Fifth Amendment Tour); *Soul Train* (Turnstyle No 1 tour); *The Winslow Boy* (Birmingham Rep/ West Yorkshire Playhouse). Future projects: *Great Expectations* (Derby Playhouse/Philadelphia USA) and *La Traviata* (English Touring Opera).

Gregory Clarke
Sound Designer

Training: Lancaster University. Gregory has engineered and operated sound extensively in the West End, on tour and internationally, including projects for the Almeida Theatre, Hampstead Theatre, Adventures in Motion Pictures, Yvonne Arnaud Theatre Guildford, Donmar Warehouse, Young Vic Theatre, English Shakespeare Company, Really Useful Group, Cameron Macintosh, The Royal National Theatre and The Royal Shakespeare Company. Gregory has also worked on the national tours of *Blood Brothers, Crazy for You, Summer Holiday, Fame, Tommy* and *Saturday Night Fever.* Recent Sound Design credits include: *The Hackney Office* (Druid Theatre, Galway); *Beyond A Joke* (Yvonne Arnaud Theatre, co-design with John Leonard); *Semi-Detatched, Pal Joey, Heartbreak House, Small Family Business* (Chichester Festival Theatre); *Snake, Gone To LA, Terracotta, Local Boy* and *Buried Alive* (Hampstead Theatre); *Dumped, A Midsummer Night's Dream* (National Youth Theatre); *The Cherry Orchard, Demons and Dybbuks and The Black Dahlia* (Method and Madness); *1999 Channel 4 Sitcom Festival* (Riverside Studios); *Nymph Errant, Song Of Singapore* (Minerva Theatre, Chichester*); Dick Whittington* (Stratford East at Greenwich); *Loves Labour's Lost* (Regent's Park); *Song Of Singapore* (May Fair Theatre, London). Gregory also re-designed the sound for the Royal Shakespeare Company's UK tour of *Tantalus.*

Vince Herbert
Lighting Designer

Vince's career has taken him to the New Shakespeare Company, Theatre Projects Consultants and the Redgrave Theatre in Farnham. He joined the Royal Exchange Theatre, Manchester as Head of Lighting in 1987 and designed the lighting there for *American Bagpipes* (which transferred to the Hampstead Theatre, London), *The Odd Couple, She Stoops To Conquer* (which toured around Great Britain following the Manchester run), *Donny Boy, Pride & Prejudice* (which also toured around the country in the Royal Exchange's Mobile Theatre), *Blythe Spirit, The Miser* (in Manchester and on tour), *The Moonstone, The Brothers Karamazov, Maybe, The Count Of Monte Cristo, Look Back In Anger, Unidentified Human Remains And The True Nature Of Love, Private Lives, Miss Julie, Animal Crackers* and most recently, *Hindle Wakes, The Philadelphia Story* and *Lady Windermere's Fan*. He also designed *Fast Food* by the same author as *Tender*. Other work includes *La Cenerentola* in Vienna, *Mother Tongue* at Greenwich, *Il Seraglio* for Scottish Opera and *Acis* and *Galatea* in Manchester Cathedral, the national tours of *Blood Brothers, Silhouette, The Importance Of Being Earnest, Vertigo* and the ill-fated *Accused* staring Jeffery Archer. Vince is now Head of Lighting at the Royal Shakespeare Company.

Pip Minnithorpe
Assistant Director

Pip graduated from the University of Birmingham in 1999. His fringe directing credits include *Reader* (Edinburgh Fringe Festival); *Attempts on her Life* (Crescent Studio); *Locked* (new, Artsfest); *Strange Encounters* (new, REP Women); *Snow* (new, MAC). Most recently Pip wrote *rom.com* and co-directed *A Tale of Many* by Jessica Maja Wild for Transmissions Young Writers Festival (The Door). Pip is Assistant Director at Birmingham Repertory Theatre courtesy of the John Fernald Award.

^{THE}REP

Birmingham Repertory Theatre

Birmingham Repertory Theatre is one of Britain's leading national theatre companies. From its base in Birmingham, The REP produces over twenty new productions each year. In October 1999 The REP completed a £7.5 million refurbishment which has transformed the theatre, renewed vital stage equipment, increased access and improved public areas.

The commissioning and production of new work lies at the core of The REP's programme. In 1998 the company launched The Door, a venue dedicated to the production and presentation of new work. This, together with an investment of almost £1 million over four years in commissioning new drama from some of Britain's brightest and best writing talent, gives The REP a unique position in British theatre. Indeed, through the extensive commissioning of new work The REP is providing vital opportunities for the young and emerging writing talent that will lead the way in the theatre of the future. Last season included new plays from Nigel Moffatt (*Musical Youth*), Jonathan Harvey (*Out in the Open*) and Sarah Daniels (*Morning Glory*). This season we look forward to this latest play by Abi Morgan, *Tender,* and Birmingham-born Gurpreet Kaur Bhatti's first play, *Behsharam* (*Shameless*).

REP productions regularly transfer to London and also tour nationally and internationally. In the last 24 months nine of our productions have been seen in London including *Two Pianos, Four Hands, Baby Doll*, *My Best Friend*, *Terracotta*, *The Gift*, *The Snowman*, *A Wedding Story, Out In The Open* and *The Ramayana* at The Royal National Theatre. Our production of *Hamlet* also played in repertoire with *Twelfth Night* on a major UK tour last year and in August played in the grounds of Elsinore Castle, Denmark as part of their annual Shakespeare Festival.

The REP's new Artistic Director, Jonathan Church, joined the company from Hampstead Theatre and his first productions, of Noël Coward's *Private Lives* in repertoire with Patrick Marber's *Closer*, open at The REP in late September.

Theatre for the world. Made in Birmingham.
www.birmingham-rep.co.uk

Artistic Director Jonathan Church
Chief Executive John Stalker
Literary Manager Ben Payne

Providing Theatre for Birmingham

European Community

European Regional Development Fund

Hampstead Theatre

Founded forty years ago, Hampstead Theatre is a small and intimate theatre, dedicated to new writing.

Our programming is diverse, accessible and contemporary, and our current annual programme of ten to twelve productions takes place against a background of extensive educational work and the reading of up to eighteen hundred plays. Through encouraging, guiding and sustaining talent, our new writing policy has a vital, national role. In fact many plays that have enjoyed successes elsewhere have often been developed and nurtured by Hampstead Theatre.

In the past twelve years alone we have presented one hundred and twenty-three plays. Thirty-six of these have gone on to a further life in the West End or on tour; actors and writers in the shows have earned between them thirty-five awards and there have been numerous spin-offs from film, television and foreign productions.

Some of the most recent plays that have had a further life include: *Someone Who'll Watch Over Me* by Frank McGuinness, *Dead Funny* by Terry Johnson, *The Memory of Water* by Shelagh Stephenson, *Little Malcolm and His Struggle Against the Eunuchs* by David Halliwell, *Peggy For You* by Alan Plater and *Feelgood* by Alistair Beaton.

In Autumn 2002 a new chapter of Hampstead Theatre's forty year story will begin: a new theatre is being built to replace our old and dilapidated portacabin. Thanks to a National Lottery grant and our own fundraising efforts an exciting translucent structure housing an ecliptical auditorium is rapidly emerging from a new site in Swiss Cottage. This new theatre will enable us to increase our work with schools and with the local neighbourhood, and of course, ensure that our essential duty to the fostering of new writing continues.

To find out more about the new theatre, or for details of how to submit a play to us, or even to keep abreast of our new productions, visit our web site at www.hampstead-theatre.co.uk.

Artistic Director Jenny Topper
Executive Director James Williams
Associate Director Jennie Darnell
Literary Manager Jeanie O'Hare

Hampstead Theatre
98 Avenue Road
Swiss Cottage
London NW3 3EX
Tel: 020 7722 9301
Fax: 020 7722 3860

PLYMOUTH THEATRE ROYAL

The Theatre Royal Plymouth opened in 1982 and in 19 years has built up a reputation as one of the largest and best attended regional theatres in the UK. The Theatre Royal attracts more than 300,000 visitors a year and in the year 2000 welcomed 24,000 *new* patrons through its doors.

The Theatre Royal regularly produces and co-produces some of the biggest and most innovative work in the UK. Recent successes which have transferred to the West End include *Buddy*, *Fame* and *Jolson*, all co-produced with E&B Productions, *Hamlet* and *Long Day's Journey Into Night*, both with the Young Vic, and *West Side Story* and the multi-award winning *Spend Spend Spend*, both co-productions with Pola Jones. The Theatre Royal produces a number of drama premieres each year including recently *Silence*, co-produced with Birmingham Repertory Theatre, *Hijra*, with the Bush Theatre, Frank Wedekind's *Musik* and *Buried Alive*, a co-production with Hampstead Theatre.

In 2001 the Theatre Royal has co-produced Ben Elton's *Inconceivable* with the West Yorkshire Playhouse, the World Stage Premiere of *Peggy Sue Got Married*, a new musical co-produced with Paul Elliott, and has been the launch venue for the touring productions of *Fosse* and *Sunset Boulevard*.

In 2002 the Theatre Royal will open a purpose built Production & Education Centre providing unrivalled creative, construction and rehearsal facilities for its productions as well as a cultural resource for the people of the South West.

Chief Executive Adrian Vinken
Artistic Director Simon Stokes
General Manager Alan Finch
Technical Director Ed Wilson

First published in 2001 by Oberon Books Ltd.
(incorporating Absolute Classics)
521 Caledonian Road, London N7 9RH
Tel: 020 7607 3637 / Fax: 020 7607 3629
e-mail: oberon.books@btinternet.com

A catalogue record for this book is available from the British
Library.

ISBN: 1 84002 238 8

Cover design: Oberon Books

Cover Image: lpp

Printed in Great Britain by Antony Rowe Ltd, Reading.

Characters

TASH
late 20s/early 30s

SQUEAL
late 20s/early mid 30s

HEN
early 30s

GLORIA
mid/late 40s

MARVIN
late 40s/early 50s

NATHAN
mid/late 30s

AL
mid/late 30s

The play is set in a city.
There are several locations.

for Jacob

Scene 1

Flat, London. Dawn light. SQUEAL in ladies dressing gown, late 20s, peering into a fridge. A wall. A window. Nothing else. TASH, late 20s, enters in towel and shower cap.

TASH: Back. Second shelf.

SQUEAL: (*Sniffing carton.*) It's off.

TASH: I'm making cheese.

SQUEAL: It doesn't matter.

TASH: It was a joke. (*Beat.*) I don't eat breakfast…

SQUEAL: Squeal…

TASH: Right… Squeal?

SQUEAL: Yeah.

TASH: Weird.

SQUEAL: As in pig.

TASH: Let's try and keep the magic shall we… (*Beat.*) How did you…?

SQUEAL: I was just in the pub and someone said party at…

TASH: (*Pointing to self.*) Veronica's.

SQUEAL: Veronica's

TASH: My name.

SQUEAL: Liar.

TASH: You been reading my post?

SQUEAL: Only the junk mail, *Veronica*.

TASH: Keep your snout out, *Squeal*.

TASH lights a fag. Opens the window and perches on the sill. He stares at her. Too long.

SQUEAL: (*Gesturing to fridge.*) Some of the stuff in here…

TASH: Don't tell me…

SQUEAL: What do you live on…

TASH: High finance.

SQUEAL: Yeah?

TASH: I'm actually a broker. There's only two women on our board of directors and you're looking at one of them.

SQUEAL: You never would have –

TASH: I don't look the type do I? I hate the way people make assumptions. Air Nike trainers, you must be Soho in media; suit, shirt and matching metallic tie, you're something stylish in high finance. It's all a load of…

SQUEAL: …guessed –

TASH: …bollocks. You know what I mean. And then everyone thinks why then has she never got any money –

SQUEAL: …considering everything that you said last –

TASH: …but it costs a fortune to buy anywhere in London even if it is in some rundown Kosher ghetto with no tube line and a hiding to –

SQUEAL: …last night…Tash –

TASH is finally silenced.

We didn't do anything.

Silence.

TASH: You can go home now.

SQUEAL: Nothing last night. Alright? Okay?

A long silence. SQUEAL stares at her. Too long.

Fine.

SQUEAL exits. TASH stubs her fag out on the window sill, thinking on this.

TASH: (*Calling out to him.*) You take it too seriously.

SQUEAL comes back, dressed and putting his shoes on.

You need to work at the pump 'em and dump 'em bit.

SQUEAL continues to ignore her.

(*A long beat.*) Nothing?

SQUEAL: Nothing.

TASH: (*Beat.*) I'm glad. (*Seeing his face.*) I don't mean to…

SQUEAL: It's nice to meet someone so –

TASH: Honest.

SQUEAL: It's not as if we're – fourteen –

TASH: I wish.

SQUEAL: You're making me feel –

TASH: Say it.

SQUEAL: (*Beat.*) …like not asking you for that second date.

As SQUEAL reaches for his coat, zipping it up and getting ready to go.

TASH: Yuri Gagarin. First man on the moon. I remember.

SQUEAL continues to get ready, reaching for a motorbike helmet.

And then we talked about oceans of water in the space between stars, the kind of soppy bollocks you talk. Squeal is that really your name?

SQUEAL: Yes. Most people call me –

TASH: (*Cutting in.*) And –

SQUEAL: And?

TASH: And you told me about trying to get in the RAF as a fighter pilot at seventeen only they found out you were colour blind and green and red are pretty bloody important if you're going to stop or go and miss a mountain. The joke about the mountain, it was funny. And you cried for a week and I said… 'Great pull line, get the girl everytime…' See. I don't forget. Then after the party…which was wild…you came on to me… I fought you off… You said when are we going to fuck. I burst into tears. My mate, Hen said… I looked like white trailer trash but it was a fucking fantastic party… Wasn't it?

SQUEAL: I was in the pub and someone said, 'Party at Veronica's.' But you weren't going. So I hung about and we came back and we talked and you drank and…

TASH: And?

SQUEAL: That's it. No fucking fantastic party. (*Beat.*) Do you want to go out with me again?

TASH: No.

SQUEAL: Right.

TASH: I'll make some tea.

SQUEAL: Milk's off.

TASH goes over and opens the fridge.

TASH: Have a drink.

SQUEAL: No thanks.

TASH: Have something. You don't have to go.

SQUEAL: What else is there?

TASH: Stay.

SQUEAL: Is this what you do? I stay, you want me to leave. I leave, you try to keep conversation going.

TASH: Hey, we've just met.

SQUEAL: And you think I'm a mug.

TASH: I don't.

SQUEAL: Yeah you do. That's fine. A one night stand is fine but –

TASH: But?

SQUEAL: I liked last night. Why don't we –

TASH: No. I like it like this. Have breakfast?

SQUEAL: You don't eat it.

TASH: I could make an exception.

SQUEAL: You started this.

TASH: Where?

SQUEAL: On a train.

TASH: Tube.

SQUEAL: It's dangerous, I could have been…

TASH: I started this on a tube…

SQUEAL: On a tube giving me the eye…

TASH: That is a matter of opinion.

SQUEAL: Giving me the eye…

TASH: A matter of…

SQUEAL: …and wanting me to follow you.

A long beat.

It was a long walk to that pub. I didn't just go for a drink.

TASH: You enjoyed. I thought you enjoyed…

SQUEAL: The intimacy of strangers?

TASH: Stay and we'll have some tea and –

SQUEAL: We'll talk about planets and things we care about and I'll make you laugh and sometime very probably as we're really sobering up, you'll cry and I might get a feel and for a moment I'll be everything you want –

SQUEAL stops himself saying something.

TASH: (*Beat.*) You've done this before?

Silence.

SQUEAL: Look at yourself.

He exits.

TASH: Thanks for nothing… (*Calling after him.*) And then what?

TASH watches him go; goes to the fridge, takes out the milk, sniffs it.

Scene 2

Office, London. Morning. A table, two chairs. The sounds of the street outside. HEN, late 20s and pregnant, is sitting patiently in front of a word processor as GLORIA, late 40s, stares into space. A long pause.

GLORIA: I've done this –

HEN: Yes –

GLORIA: I've had to do this several times before.

HEN: Yeah, I know. I bet it's –

GLORIA: Frustrating?

HEN: It would drive me –

GLORIA: It does. It is.

HEN: It's just that going through it all again, might jog something else and gives me a chance to get to know your case.

GLORIA: You're new?

HEN nods. Silence

HEN: Take your time.

GLORIA: Tall. Six feet two. Thinning hair, probably greyer now. Blue eyes. Grey suit. With navy mac and briefcase. Obviously things will have changed by now but –

HEN: Obviously.

GLORIA: Date of birth. Fifteenth November 50. Scorpio. Managed own dry cleaning firm. Parents both dead. No family except one cousin, he never really saw. Liked walking, bird watching, odd bit of football. One scar. Thumb. Bread knife. Nearly cut his finger off. Should have got a stitch.

HEN: That's significant.

GLORIA: It's the insignificance of it all actually.

HEN: Right –

GLORIA: I've had eleven months already of this.

Silence.

HEN: It was a normal day?

GLORIA: Sorry.

HEN: Nothing out of the usual? The insignificance of it all?

Silence.

I don't mean to offend you, Mrs…

23

GLORIA: Gloria.

HEN: Gloria… I just meant Mr Tate, Marvin, hadn't said anything out of the ordinary? Nothing alerted you to your husband's disappearance…

GLORIA: That doesn't mean it was as a normal day…

HEN: Of course.

GLORIA: It could never be a normal day. The colour is too bright, the sound turned up too loud and every smell and taste of that day is –

GLORIA stops herself, it's still physical this pain.

HEN: Imprinted in your mind.

Silence.

GLORIA: Re-lived.

GLORIA looks to HEN. Silence.

HEN: I see. Of course.

GLORIA: Do you get training for this job?

HEN: Yes. I'm training at the moment. They need volunteers.

Silence.

Over ten thousand people go missing every year… fifty-seven per cent of them come back within the first twenty-four hours.

GLORIA: And the other four thousand and…?

GLORIA looks at her, looks away, resumes her stare out of the window.

One month more and it will be a year.

Silence.

I don't want to start counting the anniversaries.

Silence.

I'd like to see the other woman. I normally see the one with glass –

HEN: I'm her cover.

GLORIA: You know I go through this every month? You should have the same people. It's very distressing. It isn't exactly a good advertisement is it? Missing persons and every time you show up the staff have disappeared.

HEN: We're dependent on volunteers. We tend to find people move on if they…

GLORIA: Don't have a vocation?

HEN: Feel they're unable to work within the strictures of the job. Our funds are quite low. There's only so much we can do without…

GLORIA: Any visible signs of a crime, misadventure or injury.

HEN stops, takes GLORIA in.

HEN: We're happy to co-operate with the police but we don't actually receive any financial support…

GLORIA: Without a full scale investigation.

HEN looks up from typing.

GLORIA: You've got to do something to kill the time.

A long beat.

HEN: Children?

GLORIA: Not really.

HEN: Sorry?

GLORIA: That's a blessing.

HEN: I didn't mean –

GLORIA: Why have any more people in pain?

HEN: Mrs…

GLORIA: Gloria.

HEN: Gloria… Are you having counselling?

Silence. GLORIA almost laughs.

GLORIA: I find swimming helps…

HEN: That sounds good.

GLORIA: He didn't like chlorine. I never went but now…
  Something good has come out of something bad.

HEN: Exactly.

GLORIA: Are you going to put that down? About the
  swimming…

HEN: I don't think it's…

GLORIA: Because perhaps if you could release that sort of
  information… I've also decorated the hallway. Citrus
  colours. He liked blues… It might encourage him to
  come home…

HEN: Gloria…

GLORIA: If he knows the full extent I am going to make
  my life tick over. Move on. Keep going. That I'm not a
  responsibility then maybe he'd want to come back…

HEN: A lot of people…

GLORIA: Blame themselves and ask whether there is
  something they could have done?

HEN: Exactly…They feel that…

GLORIA: I was a fantastic wife…

HEN: I'm sure…

GLORIA: The house was always clean, I ironed shirts. I use to even run him a bath. It's old fashioned but it's what I did…

HEN: It must be impossible to make sense of why he would just go like that…

GLORIA: I try to make sense of it every day. Saturday was our shopping day and Sunday's we'd often go to the neighbours… People don't often get on with their neighbours… I get on with mine… We got…get on with ours…

HEN: Being on your own is very daunting –

GLORIA: You know that?

HEN: If you were married for… (*Reading screen.*) …twenty-two years…

GLORIA: Twenty-three Monday…

HEN: Partners often find in the period of readjustment that…

GLORIA: Please. Don't talk to me like that.

Silence.

I'm actually starting to enjoy it, that's the fear… I'm actually finding that it is becoming normal and that's what I find frightening… That's what worries me most… That if he did come back, maybe I wouldn't want… That's why I think it's so important that you release that kind of information… Like I've done the garden and the back wall was coming down but John from next door has helped me fix it and that you just get on. I'm not helpless. If he knows that. That I'm stopping needing him… I think he'll come back…

HEN: I don't think I can help you here.

GLORIA: There's a slot on TV. With music and they show pictures of people missing. People in Christmas hats, slightly pissed people or tired people with rucksacks, at parties or hugging their mum, and it's the ones who are left who they should show pictures of. Photos of them smiling and on holiday and waving a flag. Photos that say they don't need them. That might jog some memory in the mind of those who have gone. That they had a family and responsibilities…

HEN: Gloria…

GLORIA: That they don't go to bed at night anymore wondering where they are. That at last they have found peace…

HEN: If that were true you wouldn't be here.

GLORIA: Have you ever been left?

HEN: Gloria, I understand how you must be…

GLORIA: Have you?

HEN's silence says it all.

Then how do you know…

A long silence.

HEN: If I could just take down some more details.

Silence.

GLORIA: How many weeks…until your baby?

HEN: A few yet.

GLORIA: That's good. That's lovely. A new life. Congratulations.

HEN: Thanks very much.

GLORIA: That's quite alright.

GLORIA looks to HEN. Holds her stare. HEN returns to typing.

Scene 3

Loud bar. London. TASH is standing, suit on, glass in hand. Bright lights. Abstract painting. HEN sits gripped, orange juice in hand.

TASH: And I'm in this bar and I see him and because at that exact moment I am the most interesting woman in the place who understands him. Then I have to go over and say, 'Wotcha' and then I see who he's with and she's really bloody famous and you'd know her…you know that woman who's in that…we saw it…with the…

HEN: Fuck –

TASH: 'Superb' I say… 'You were so gorgeous in that… It made me and my friend cry.' And she's all fluffy and preening herself at this and I say, 'I love you…' And him, fucking famous arty tough looking fart who I will not repeat…

HEN: Get on with it –

TASH: For fear, he'll stuff me in a tank and pickle me as 'Fucking Pissed Cow dribbling all over my bit of squeeze.' He looks at me, so fucking mean he was and he says, 'Go Away' – in a monotone bloody Babylon 5 android sort of way and I…

HEN: Because you're pissed…

TASH: Because I'm pissed and because I've powdered my nose far too many times for me to truly justify any intellectual conversation, proceed to tell him just how boring I would find myself and what is he doing here? Because shouldn't he be at home with his wife and child. And I've really hit a nerve now…

HEN: Tash… What made you say? What made you say –

TASH: 'Go away.' And he pushes me on the shoulder so I push him…

HEN: You stupid fucking…

TASH: And we end up playing this pat a cake, pat a cake, melarky and I'm getting more embarrassing and will not leave them alone. I'm like a limpet, clinging…and I'm not a clingy person…am I?

HEN: No. You? No.

TASH: So they get up to go and of course I have to follow because I'm with Magda –

HEN: Bad girl.

TASH: Great girl. Very good for me. I'm with Magda and she's saying 'Who?' And I say… Fart art who puts things in pickle stuff and she's reeling now because she's copped off with Ben behind the bar who's feeding her Sea Breezes through a drip and cutting up her own lines on the till and so we have to find him…

HEN: Tash…

TASH: Don't get like that… So she's dragging me around but I've forgotten him by then and I'm just preying he's forgotten me so I sit myself down with this tall guy and I keep saying 'So what's your name?' 'Paul…' 'And what do you do?' 'I'm a popstar.' 'So what's your name?' 'Paul…' 'And what do you do?' 'So what's your name…?' 'Paul and I'm a fucking famous pop star,' and he tells me who, that band, fucking elevator music, what is that band, anyway he tells me the name of the band and I say, 'Aren't you meant to be black?' which pisses him off something chronic and I say, 'Look I'm sorry' and I can't seem to leave him alone and I tell him I'd be bored with him if he was me and then I say…

HEN: You didn't…

TASH: I pull out my trump card, the one that normally always gets them… Because I'm off my rocks the way I was at…

HEN: Diane's wedding…

TASH: …And by this time I am almost dribbling all over the carpet… I say to him… 'Look I'm off my tits. I've been tied up and drugged and made to take copious amounts of alcohol I didn't really want…don't be rude to me… Imagine if I was your mother… Imagine if I was your sister.' And this is it… This is the big whammy, Hen… Are you ready for it? Look like it then… 'Imagine I was your sister…' And he looks at me, this super big pop star and for the first time I see him, I recognise him and I look around and the place is crawling with Jack shit celebs and me and he says… 'My sister wouldn't degrade herself like you.'

HEN: (*Beat.*) Oow…

TASH knocks back her drink. A pained silence.

TASH: You know…It happens. You get over it but I tell you I still can't listen to their music without feeling physically sick.

HEN: I'm sorry.

TASH: See that's why I wasn't going to tell you. Because I knew you'd get upset.

HEN: I'm only saying.

TASH: It's a story. It's designed to amuse.

HEN: It still must have hurt.

TASH: You see that's when I really question our friendship. When you try to do that 'let's tap into the soft underbelly of her mind,' time. It was a laugh. I told you to make you laugh.

HEN: It is funny.

TASH: Then why aren't you laughing? Fat cow.

HEN: Pickled cow.

TASH: It was the drugs…I'd hardly touched a drop.

HEN: That makes it better? Jesus Tash – So?

TASH: What? What are you drinking?

HEN: I'm alright. The other night?

TASH: You're not fucking drinking.

HEN: I'm alright. It's so fucking loud here. Why do you always want to meet where it's so bloody loud?

TASH: I can't wait for you to shit that watermelon. You're boring without a drink in you.

HEN: I'll be up all night. Tash –

TASH: Al keeping you busy.

HEN: Hah, yeah. Al's knackered, he's working on that site, you know that big site –

TASH: How would I know a big fuck off building site?

HEN: Funny. Very funny. We need the money.

TASH: Is that why you're slaving over a hot computer?

HEN: I enjoy my job. I'm doing something worthwhile.

TASH: And I'm not?

HEN: I didn't mean that…But while we're talking about it –

TASH: Fuck off –

HEN: You never settle –

TASH: I'm a late developer.

HEN: You never settle anywhere for more than a few weeks.

TASH: Who would…who would serve deep fried Mars Bars –

HEN: You got yourself into that job –

TASH: …stay longer than a few weeks…days… I do do…I can do skilled work. I just challenge, getting into the job then –

HEN: Shagging your way out.

TASH: (*Beat.*) What is the crime, I don't see the crime in that?

HEN: What is it… Today… You're so defensive. (*Beat.*) You copped off the other night.

TASH: I'm always copping off the other night. Have a little one? Go on…Why not?

HEN: It stunts the growth.

TASH: Mental growth of the mother if she can't knock back the odd glass of…

HEN: Will you please… Red wine. One glass.

TASH: That a girl!

TASH nods to a waiter. Silence.

I could kill him. I could honestly kill him. This wasn't meant to happen.

HEN: Will you get over it? I've been with him six years.

TASH: And you were not meant to get pregnant. It's such a cliché.

HEN: You're avoiding the subject.

TASH: I had a fuck. Doctor. Bit lame with his hands. Which is disappointing in a man of medicine. Haven't seen him since the deed. Nothing much to add.

HEN: And I was hoping.

TASH: No please. Shall we go on?

HEN: No. I don't want to get too tired. I promised Al. He worries.

TASH: You promised Al. (*Beat.*) I like Al. I love Al. He's like a brother to me.

HEN: You just get like that. More protectful. More aware… There was a time I would just step out on a zebra crossing even if…especially if I saw a car. I figured the insurance policy would pay for the new leg and the holiday of a life time. It would be worth it but now…

TASH: When you get like this it leaves me cold. I'm sorry.

HEN: You're getting worse.

TASH: I'm definitely getting worse.

HEN: You should have got use to it by now.

TASH: It's a shock.

HEN: What?

TASH: That you're settling… You're choosing to settle. You're having your future now.

Silence.

It's gorgeous. It's lovely…

HEN: It's normal. Women of our age have children. It's a good age.

TASH: For doing something with your life.

HEN: I don't remember that being single was so great.

TASH: Oow.

HEN: (*Beat.*) Sorry.

TASH: Point deserved. If I could be like you. I don't chose this –

HEN: Yes you do. You could if you wanted.

TASH: Could I? How do you do it? You know I watch people on tubes and in the street, couples together, and I think how do they do it… Ring each other, keep seeing each other, keep wanting to be together, eat enough meals, and share enough Christmas' to justify that they are no longer single.

HEN: You're too –

TASH: Don't say choosy. People always say choosy when what they really think is –

HEN: Perhaps they didn't browse long enough?

TASH: I like Al.

HEN: I like Al.

TASH: *Like*?

HEN: I *love* Al.

They drink.

This woman was in work today. Typical case. Husband had just walked out, nearly a year ago now. Paid up the mortgage, fed the cat, dry-cleaned his suit, saw she was alright, discussed with her what he'd like for his tea, left the house and just didn't bother coming back. Maybe that's what happens. Maybe you just pick something up, wear it for a while and then put it down. For most of us death or some other woman gets there before that decision is made but for some people…

TASH: You never know someone. You think you do but one day you look up and – I'm just not romantic.

HEN: Yes you are. You could have whoever you want.

TASH: Yeah, yeah, yeah… The pick up is the easy part. It's the staying with, I can't get a taste for.

HEN: What's his name?

TASH: The service is shite here.

HEN: Don't tell me…you didn't even get his name… Tash…

TASH: Squeal… His name's Squeal.

HEN: As in pig?

TASH: Yeah.

HEN: Sounds good.

TASH: Sounds nothing.

HEN: You just don't trust men.

TASH: Please. Cliché.

Silence.

I'm sorry it's just – children aren't everything.

Silence.

You alright?

HEN: (*Beat.*) Laughing.

TASH: (*Long beat.*) Do you know there are oceans of water between the stars and the moon?

Scene 4

Outdoor pool. London. GLORIA sitting on the side of a swimming pool, in costume, goggles and hat as SQUEAL stands in trunks, drying himself with a towel. GLORIA suddenly flinches.

GLORIA: Christ.

SQUEAL: Are you okay?

GLORIA: I've been… (*She cranes around, trying to see over her shoulder, feeling her back.*) …stung.

SQUEAL: It's the start of the lazy wasps. They get lazy waking up –

GLORIA: And I'm dinner. Oow.

SQUEAL: You need vinegar.

GLORIA: Serves me right for just sitting.

SQUEAL makes to go.

You're a very good swimmer.

SQUEAL: It's a bit cold today to be honest.

GLORIA: I used to come here as a girl.

SQUEAL: Yeah?

GLORIA: Hasn't been decorated since. They're all very colourful here aren't they? All the people.

SQUEAL: I guess.

GLORIA: It's my daily ritual. I sit here.

SQUEAL: You don't swim…

GLORIA: Not really… If it's hot I might have a dip but… I just enjoy the sunshine and the people. You get to remembering faces.

SQUEAL: Uh huh.

GLORIA: (*Beat.*) That's how I remember yours.

SQUEAL nods, smiles, turns to go.

You're a lawyer.

SQUEAL: Sorry?

GLORIA: In the city. You look like a lawyer.

SQUEAL: No –

GLORIA: I sometimes get it wrong. I sit and try and work out what people do.

GLORIA rubs her shoulder.

SQUEAL: It'll pass soon.

GLORIA: Little buggers.

SQUEAL nods, makes to go.

Teaching then?

SQUEAL: Doctor.

GLORIA: Of course. You've got the hands of a doctor.

SQUEAL: People always say –

GLORIA: It's true.

SQUEAL: People always say that.

GLORIA: My husband has the hands of a dry cleaner. They're soft but very red from all the fluid –

SQUEAL: He should wear –

GLORIA: I tell him.

SQUEAL: He should wear gloves. You tell him.

GLORIA: Doctor's orders. He says it keeps them soft. For wetting the ring of pint glasses. He wets them and rings them… He always knows it makes me laugh.

SQUEAL: (*Beat.*) Still –

GLORIA: Still –

SQUEAL makes to go.

GLORIA: What kind of doctor?

SQUEAL: Casualty. I'm a houseman. I'm just in casualty at the moment.

GLORIA: But you're helping people. That means something.

SQUEAL: Yeah, sewing up knife wounds and mopping up drunks.

GLORIA: Your family must be very –

SQUEAL: Just my dad. Yeah, he thinks it's alright.

GLORIA: He must be very proud. A doctor.

SQUEAL: No –

GLORIA: A doctor is what every one wants in the family.

SQUEAL: He doesn't say much. I never know.

GLORIA: He will be.

SQUEAL: You think? (*Beat.*) He has a bad heart.

GLORIA: That's no excuse. Make sure he tells you.

SQUEAL: Okay…

GLORIA: Gloria.

SQUEAL: I'll tell him, Gloria.

GLORIA: You tell him. People don't appreciate each other enough.

Silence. SQUEAL picks up his wet towel, turns to go.

SQUEAL: You should have a swim. It's great once you get in.

GLORIA: Too chilly for me today...

SQUEAL: You always just sit?

GLORIA: You been watching me?

SQUEAL: It's a waste of a ticket.

GLORIA: Giving me the eye.

SQUEAL: It must be a couple of quid a day. You'd be as good sitting by the pond than...

GLORIA: (*Sharp.*) It's company.

Silence. SQUEAL hovers.

Sometimes conversation. I fall into conversation. I met a woman last week who'd lost an eye.

SQUEAL: That was careless.

GLORIA: Cricket bat in the eye. She said it gave her a whole different perspective.

SQUEAL: It would.

GLORIA: Losing an eye like that. (*Beat.*) You probably see that all the time.

SQUEAL: It's still a shock.

GLORIA: Yeah.

SQUEAL: Still would take some getting use to.

GLORIA: Yeah. (*Beat.*) How would you put your mascara on?

A half ripple of laughter. SQUEAL hovers.

SQUEAL: Right… Okay… Vinegar on that wasp sting.

GLORIA: I can't even feel it.

SQUEAL: Bye then…

As SQUEAL turns to go.

GLORIA: I can't swim… I can doggy paddle a bit but –

SQUEAL: That's a start.

GLORIA: Marvin was fantastic swimmer. I wonder now why I never… I just sit at the side.

SQUEAL: You should give it a go.

GLORIA: I don't like to get my ears wet.

SQUEAL: They do classes.

GLORIA: I'd hold everyone back.

SQUEAL: I saw a big man must have been about eighteen stone and he was learning the other week…

GLORIA: I'd be their first drowning.

SQUEAL: You'd float.

GLORIA: Not me. I'd sink to the bottom.

SQUEAL: No you wouldn't.

GLORIA: How do you know?

SQUEAL: Well whatever.

GLORIA: Yeah whatever.

SQUEAL: Breast stroke's easy.

GLORIA: I'm sure…

SQUEAL: Dead easy… I could…

GLORIA: What?

SQUEAL hovers.

SQUEAL: I better get off. Careful you don't roast. Your shoulders look...

GLORIA: Yes...

SQUEAL: They're's nothing to be frightened of. Lifeguards all round the edge and people everywhere to save you.

GLORIA: (*Almost to herself.*) A doctor.

SQUEAL: Bye, Gloria.

SQUEAL makes to go.

GLORIA: He should look at you and say I'm proud you're my son.

SQUEAL: Squeal.

GLORIA: The runt of the litter.

SQUEAL: Yeah. (*He hesitates and turns back.*) Gloria...

GLORIA: Yeah.

SQUEAL: If you want...

GLORIA: Yes.

SQUEAL: If you'd let me...

GLORIA: Please.

SQUEAL: Breast stroke's the easiest one to get.

GLORIA turns, smiles. Holds his stare. Too long. She tentatively nods her head.

Scene 5

Supermarket, South London. AL is wheeling a shopping trolley. HEN is ahead, contemplating the cereals.

HEN: So you never wonder?

AL: Nah?

HEN: You never imagine for one moment what it might have been like if it had been someone else?

AL: It wasn't. It was you.

HEN: So you think it's fate.

AL: It's choice. You have a choice as to how you live your life. Some are good at it, some are crap.

HEN: So you chose me.

AL: Not exactly. There are random moments and moments of decision. You were a moment of decision following a random event.

HEN: We've been together for the last six years. What's random about that?

AL: It wasn't planned. Getting pregnant was a random event.

HEN: And you think that's what makes up life?

AL: We came to buy some cereal. You said you were hungry and it had to be cereal.

HEN: We were drunk.

AL: Random moment.

HEN: Choice to keep it?

AL: Moment of decision.

HEN: And you think that's what makes up life?

AL: I don't know. I'm a builder.

HEN: So.

AL: We got peanut butter?

HEN: It's a lifetime. We are talking about a lifetime

AL: Have you been talking to Tash again?

HEN: I always talk to Tash.

AL: She's single –

HEN: So.

AL: And thirty –

HEN: Just. And that makes her bitter?

AL: It makes her stir it with her mates who have people.

HEN: You don't have me.

AL: Cheers.

HEN: Don't you ever think you have me.

AL: Alright...alright... Keep your wig on.

HEN: Sometimes you make me nervous.

AL: Right.

HEN: You can react a bit.

AL: Alright. (*Beat.*) Right.

HEN: Is that it?

AL: Hen, where you from?

HEN: Southall.

AL: Where am I from?

HEN: Southall.

AL: So what does that say?

HEN: What?

AL: What does that say?

HEN: We both know where to go to get a good curry?

AL: It says you know me. And I know you. And your dad knows where I live so if I did anything to make you nervous he doesn't have to walk far to do me one.

HEN: 'Til death us do part?

AL avoids this conversation concentrating on the cereal choice.

AL: Crunchy? (*Holding up jar.*) I'm getting crunchy.

HEN: A baby's a lifetime.

AL: Only swans mate for life.

HEN: Your cynical.

AL: Couldn't even spell it. I'm not cynical, I'm pulling your leg. I said yes. I said yes, didn't I?

HEN: This isn't just you and me. It isn't like a quickie and a phone number scribbled down on the back of your hand.

AL: It's hardly a teen cock up. We've been going six years, Hen.

HEN: I don't want to end up like Tash. I don't want to wake up and find myself on my own with a kid.

AL: She hasn't got one.

HEN: But she's on her own.

AL: There are worse things.

HEN: What are you saying?

AL: People do it. Bring up kids on their own.

HEN: Is that what you're suggesting?

AL: No. No.

HEN: You're winding me up now.

AL: We're having a baby.

HEN: And that's alright with you?

AL: I said yes.

HEN: But you've hardly thought about it.

AL: What's there to think about?

HEN: Like where we're going to live, if I'm going to give up my job, whose name he's going to have.

AL: So we've decided it's a boy then.

HEN: It's not funny. Like if you want it.

AL: Yeah, I want it.

HEN: You wouldn't have wanted to wait?

AL: Maybe a year or so but –

HEN: See –

AL: But only 'til the house was finished. I wanted us to be able to live in the house.

HEN: What are you saying? What are you saying?

AL: I'm saying if we were working to Railtrack Guidelines then maybe we might have kicked around waiting a bit longer but... Hen... We only came out to buy cereal.

HEN: Do you love me?

AL: They've got an offer on Pampers.

HEN: Do you love me?

AL: (*Beat.*) With all my heart. (*He moves off with the trolley.*) I'll get this.

HEN: (*Beat.*) I don't want to be like Tash. I don't want to be like Tash living in a shit heap, no one to love, moving from one naff job to another –

AL: Maybe she finds happiness in other ways.

Scene 6

Loft apartment, Soho, London. NATHAN is sitting in his loft apartment; modernist, Conranesque, slick in Joseph sweats, dressing gown and Nike. He butters a bagel. TASH stands videoing him.

TASH: And what exactly are you doing now?

NATHAN: I'm buttering a bagel. Then…depending on my mood, I will place a small square, leaf of smoked salmon on the top, sometimes I might slice a pickle but mostly, it's a nub of black pepper and my dark coffee which I get at Grodinski's, the FT if I feel in the mood.

TASH: And you always put the salmon on after?

NATHAN: The bagel, then the cheese, then the salmon, then the pepper.

TASH: Or the pickle.

NATHAN: The pickle if I'm in the mood or even a lemon.

TASH: Now what would I do?

NATHAN: Well you could say something like – 'Would you find it useful if perhaps, you could buy it all in one pack, cheese, bagel, salmon, pepper…?'

TASH: Lemon?

NATHAN: And the lemon. Say in one pack?

TASH: You want me to kind of think along those sort of lines?

NATHAN: The company is paid to see where the gap is in the market. To see the way people live, eat, consume. So if you can come up with any observations along the way, that's great. That's dandy.

TASH: Okay…

NATHAN: I hope you don't mind this. Doing this meeting in my flat? It's just Sundays –

TASH: Sundays. I know Sundays are sacred.

NATHAN: Most of my employees hot desk anyway. We're rarely ever in the same room at the same time. Tash. Natasha. Russian?

TASH: Croydon.

NATHAN: Try and hold the camera level if you can. It's just the clients get pissed off –

TASH: Sure –

NATHAN: Fuck it. I'm the boss. You wobble if you like? (*Beat.*) So?

TASH: So… Would you find it useful if perhaps you could buy it all in one pack, cheese, bagel, salmon, pepper, lemon?

NATHAN: It's an idea. Maybe a gimmick but I can do it myself. The enjoyment is doing it yourself. They might say something like that. You often find people initiate the opposite response if you present them with a specific idea. Remember to get them to hold up the packet of whatever they're buying to the camera. We need to show the client, to let them see their branding.

TASH: Okay… Could you hold up the lid of the cheese packet? I've just got to logo register.

NATHAN holds up the lid for the camera. TASH films it zooming in.

TASH: We're very grateful.

NATHAN: I'm happy to oblige.

TASH: We're finding logo's very important at the moment. Red's always a good colour. See a red logo on the cheese lid. It's probably what made you buy it.

NATHAN: That's great. That shows initiative, it's just a little more than you need.

TASH: Right, sorry.

NATHAN: I think you're great at this, Tash. You're spot on.

TASH: Yeah?

NATHAN: Really…really great.

NATHAN reads his paper, aware he is being filmed. He pours himself another cup of coffee, adding sugar, then pouring in a little more coffee.

TASH: Coffee…then sugar…then coffee?

NATHAN: It melts it quicker. It's a habit. Nothing else.

TASH: It's interesting.

NATHAN pours another cup and places it opposite him.

And you're pouring another cup?

NATHAN: For you.

TASH: Thanks.

NATHAN flicks through a CV as he eats and drinks.

NATHAN: You've done a lot of jobs. Your CV shows a lot of jobs.

TASH: Yeah.

NATHAN is buttering a second bagel and placing it on a plate opposite.

NATHAN: Eat.

TASH puts down the camera.

TASH: Cheers.

NATHAN: There's no harm in that. Taking your time to find what you really want to do.

TASH: Would I be doing this in people's houses?

NATHAN: Sometimes but… Mainly supermarkets, the large food chains. I go out and do it myself sometimes. That's unusual in the agency but I like to keep in touch. It makes the client feel like I really know their product.

Silence.

I spend a lot of time with housewives. They tend to be our biggest resource. I think you'll be good with them. (*Beat.*) It's quick money.

TASH: That's what I always want. I've been doing up a flat… Talking about doing up my flat. (*Beat.*) I never do. (*Beat.*) Earning money…earning money can be a motivation. (*She sniffs the coffee.*) Real.

NATHAN shrugs.

You don't look like an instant man.

TASH rests her camera on the side and sits down to take the coffee.

NATHAN: Good. Good observational skills –

Silence. NATHAN pours her another cup of coffee. TASH smiles, a little embarrassed. NATHAN smiles a little embarrassed.

TASH: You live on your own? It feels as if…

Silence.

NATHAN: (*Beat.*) It takes getting used to, living on your own. So you're interested?

TASH: Yeah…

NATHAN: Good…that's great. Well, lets get you rocking and rolling. How about starting –

TASH: Today. I could start today.

NATHAN: Tomorrow's fine just I'll walk you down just…let me take a shower.

TASH nods, flicking the camera up.

TASH: Of course. We want you just to do everything as you would normally do.

NATHAN gets up to shower.

NATHAN: You can put down the camera now.

TASH: I was just getting into it.

NATHAN eats a tangerine. TASH flicks the camera back on him.

(*Beat.*) Fruit. You always end with fruit?

NATHAN holds up the tangerine bag label up to the camera; smiling.

NATHAN: It aids digestion. See, I logo registered, Natasha.

TASH: …you do seem to have picked up the technique, Nathan.

NATHAN eats. TASH sits, stealing a bagel from his plate.

I'll walk you down.

Scene 7

A park, South London. GLORIA is sitting on a park bench with SQUEAL. They are eating sandwiches and take away drinks enjoying the sunshine. Their hair is wet. They've just been for a swim.

SQUEAL: You breathe out as you pull.

GLORIA: I drown if I breathe and I pull. I open my mouth and I drown.

SQUEAL: So you close your mouth, then you breath out through your nose.

GLORIA: That's unhealthy. That's bad for you. In through your nose, out through your mouth. Germs pass that way.

SQUEAL: You're swimming in a thousand gallons of chlorine, anything would be zapped. (*Beat.*) You're funny. You're pulling my leg.

GLORIA laughs to herself.

GLORIA: Gullible.

SQUEAL: Not in the dictionary.

GLORIA: It's so nice with the sun.

SQUEAL: Yes.

GLORIA: I feel so nice. (*Beat.*) I walked past your flat the other day.

SQUEAL: Yeah…

GLORIA: The one with the bins outside.

SQUEAL: It's good for the hospital.

GLORIA: I couldn't live without my garden.

SQUEAL: Gloria –

GLORIA: I did live with my husband but he's not there anymore.

SQUEAL: You still wear your weding ring?

GLORIA: Can't get it off.

SQUEAL: My dad still wears his.

Silence.

A garden must be great in this weather.

GLORIA: It is now. Was a state but… I've almost finished it now. Patio and a little pond near the shed. With fish. I wanted Koi carp but they're expensive. £200. Imagine paying that for a bag of fish and chips? (*Beat.*) Frogs and goldfish are just as nice. (*Beat.*) He liked fish and chips.

SQUEAL: You never had –

GLORIA: No. Marvin was always handful enough… I was never the mothering kind.

GLORIA watches something in the distance.

There are girls who take men down here and do things behind those trees, aren't there? I'm not stupid. If you sit here long enough. (*Beat.*) Good job it's summer. Maybe that's what my husband did. Maybe he use to come down here and pick up a girl and stand up against a tree and… They would have sex. And maybe one day he couldn't come back and face me with it. Maybe he knew I'd smell it on him or just know. A wife's instinct.

SQUEAL: I don't think…

GLORIA: You didn't know him. Maybe that's what he did. And maybe afterwards she would hand him her knickers and fold them into a little square and let him slip them in his pocket. And maybe he would come home and for his tea, and sit down and eat whatever I've put in front of him and all the time he'd be thinking I've got some girl's pants in my pocket. (*Beat.*) Could you never see yourself doing that if you were married?

SQUEAL: No, Gloria.

GLORIA: You say that.

SQUEAL: No.

GLORIA: Just a thought. There's a bench as well. By the pond. And John next door is going to help me build a Gazebo.

SQUEAL: Is that edible?

GLORIA: For flowers. For sitting. For sitting in and thinking. He won't recognise the place when he gets back, will he Squeal?

SQUEAL: I don't know.

GLORIA: That man…

GLORIA has not taken her eyes off someone in the distance.

…with the cap on… That man. Can you see that man? Go over. Will you… Just… Squeal… Will you… He's wearing… That cap… Like my… Please will you just look for me… Just go over and ask him…

SQUEAL: I don't know him, Gloria. I never…

GLORIA: (*With realisation.*) It's not him. (*Beat.*) It's alright. It's not him.

SQUEAL: I'm sorry.

GLORIA: I drive everyone mad. I always think…

SQUEAL puts out his hand and rests it on GLORIA's. She tentatively tightens her grip around it, stroking it.

GLORIA: I'm always wrong…

SQUEAL: Gloria…

GLORIA: Have you ever been in love?

SQUEAL: Gloria…

GLORIA: I don't mean married love. I mean love with no responsibility. Love with no expectation. Love without the cleaning and the washing shirts.

SQUEAL: Sometimes…

GLORIA loosens her grip on his hand.

GLORIA: Yes.

SQUEAL: (*Beat.*) Maybe sometimes I think I could be… I could fall…become in love with someone.

GLORIA: And her?

SQUEAL: (*Beat.*) She's a bit slower on the uptake.

A long silence as GLORIA sits clearly upset, clearly not willing to speak.

SQUEAL: You should try backstroke. Backstroke's the easiest. Next week I'll show you backstroke.

GLORIA turns and looks at him. She nods. She smiles.

GLORIA: And after I could cook your tea.

SQUEAL does not know what to say.

SQUEAL: If you want.

GLORIA: I bet you like…

SQUEAL: Everything.

The squawk of birds as SQUEAL and GLORIA both instinctively look up. The slow beat of wings as if in a flock on migration.

GLORIA: I wonder where they're going to.

Scene 8

Bar, Soho, London. TASH and HEN. Same bar. Same drinks. Same routine. Loud.

TASH: So I'm sitting there thinking this is weird, I'm sitting there seriously wondering how I'm going to get myself out of this one because I don't know if you remember but when I lived with Itkin.

HEN: The Jewish boy from hell.

TASH: I was writing the name in all the mirrors if you remember and something which I, now, as a reformed character…

HEN: Since the pickled cow incident.

TASH: Since I spilt my emotional innards out all over the carpet of that coke trodden single cracked orchid shit hole in the heart of metropolis, do not and for full velocity of that concept, do not let grace my nostrils or gums. I am not looking to get drawn into flagrante delicto with some twisted sister, battered childhood, anal retentive and other sexual deviant practising tosser, even if he does have a white peace pad in Soho. I am not looking for a shag with an emotional timebomb just waiting to explode all over my life, probably into my bank account and certainly an experience which will entail several short sharp trips to the Woman's centre, your legs up in stirrups trying to deny any knowledge of that large scaly pustule adorning your feminine minge.

HEN: You slept with him.

TASH: Excuse me. I don't spend all day listening to the rejected. He was nice… He walked me down… It's going well. The job. I'm not interested… I'm really not interested. He's obviously the kind of guy who gets dumped.

HEN: When did you get so bitter, Tash?

TASH: Sorry?

HEN: You slept with him.

AL walks in.

TASH: Alright. You coming to the –

HEN: Sorry I meant to –

TASH: No that's fine, that's great…

AL kisses HEN hello as he gestures to the waiter for a drink. TASH kisses AL.

AL: Alright Tash.

TASH: Hello gorgeous.

AL: What time's the – ?

HEN: Eight.

TASH: (*To AL.*) You won't like it. It's that thing with –

HEN: The girl who's in –

TASH: It's romantic…

HEN: Playing the monkey?

TASH: She wasn't a monkey.

HEN: They were all bloody monkeys. She was in love with –

AL: I like romantic films.

TASH: Great.

Silence.

How's the house?

AL: Put the windows in at the weekend.

HEN: Sash. They're reclaimed sash.

TASH: Nice one. I've not even stripped a wall yet.

HEN: Al could –

AL: Yeah, I could –

TASH: No, I'm alright –

HEN: We've got a steamer.

AL: It's like butter with a steamer.

TASH: I like the walls.

HEN: They're bloody awful.

TASH: They're *my* bloody awful. (*Beat.*) I like them. Cheers
    but –

AL: You're fine.

HEN: Sorry I should have –

TASH: It's fine. I guess we got the –

AL: Booby prize.

TASH: …night your mates didn't need you to sit on their
    sofas like lard, drink beer and watch football.

HEN: Nasty. Why are you two so nasty to each other?

TASH: We are lovely to each other.

AL: I didn't say a word.

HEN: We should –

TASH: We're fine.

HEN: The trailers. Al likes to watch the trailers.

AL: That's not true. It's fine.

HEN: Three's a very bad number. Three is notoriously
    difficult. Someone is always left out.

TASH: Which book are you reading now?

HEN: It's not a book. I'm just saying.

TASH: How do you live with her?

AL: Take the pills and buy in Sky sport.

TASH: You're looking very toned.

AL: I've been working a lot –

TASH: So are you going to let this one finally stop and give herself a rest?

HEN: We can go and see a film together. We can go and see a bloody film together.

TASH: You didn't mention he was coming.

HEN: It was last minute.

TASH: You should have said if you wanted to spend the evening with Al.

HEN: I wanted to spend an evening with you both. This isn't a competition.

TASH: What you talking about? (*To AL.*) Do you know what she is talking about?

HEN: You don't help yourself Tash. You don't make yourself easy.

TASH: What? I don't discuss window frames and what colour carpets and what wallpaper I need to put up on my walls and –

HEN: I don't mean that. You make it hard for people to like you.

Silence. TASH laughs. HEN laughs.

It's a bloody film. We can go and see a bloody film without it turning into full combat.

AL: Sorry.

TASH: You don't have to be sorry.

AL: I wasn't talking to you.

HEN: Al.

> *Silence.*

> Get over it you two, eh?

TASH: You want to do my decorating?

AL: If you like. With the steamer I've got, I tell you it's like cutting through –

TASH: Yeah. Okay. Thanks.

> *TASH thinks of offering some gesture of affection; instead she chinks her glass with HEN, leans forward and kisses AL on the cheek.*

AL: Hen says you've got a new job.

HEN: Market research.

AL: That's probably good money.

TASH: It's sitting looking at people's sad lives.

AL: I guess it depends how you're feeling. Everyone looks sad if you're feeling –

TASH: A bit blue? Don't say a bit blue. (*Looking to AL.*) I saw you the other week.

AL: Yeah?

TASH: Lunch hour. You were with –

AL: My boss' daughter's doing work placement.

HEN: What's her name? She's got a lovely name.

AL: If it's a girl, we're going to call her Natasha.

AL holds TASH's stare.

Like butter. I'll come over next week.

TASH: Great.

HEN: (*Beat.*) He hasn't done the job yet.

HEN breaks into a smile, pushing him affectionately as a ripple of laughter finally breaks between the three. HEN wets her finger and absently rings the top of her glass. It makes a low long hum.

Scene 9

Street, London. TASH in a hurry, dressed up. Rain. Traffic. SQUEAL running past showering under a wadge of documents, in a hurry, not slowing down.

TASH: So I was thinking –

SQUEAL: Sorry?

TASH: These oceans. Do they have fish in? Do they have whales and if that is the case, that is officially a mammal and where there are mammals there are humans, so are therefore the stars planets, with people living on them and those oceans of water are like our Atlantic?

SQUEAL: I don't know what you're –

TASH: I knew you were a bullshitter –

SQUEAL: Sorry.

TASH: If you were telling the truth, you would be pleased that I have remembered your late night ramblings and be willing to defend your theory –

SQUEAL: It's raining –

TASH: This precludes thought.

SQUEAL: (*Beat.*) Hello Tash –

TASH: I'm passed that bit. I'm mid sentence with you now –

SQUEAL: I'm on call.

TASH: Yeah, me too. Consultancy, it's the direction most people in marketing are going now –

SQUEAL: What?

TASH: So your theory is flunked.

SQUEAL: Right.

TASH: Doesn't matter.

SQUEAL: We're getting –

TASH: I hate umbrellas. I think people who carry umbrellas look too –

SQUEAL: Prepared.

TASH: – anal. I find that a big turn off.

SQUEAL: I don't carry one. Do you?

TASH: Do you? Sorry. You go.

SQUEAL: Coffee. Do you want a get a coffee?

TASH: No.

SQUEAL: Okay.

TASH: I'm –

SQUEAL: Sure. Definitely.

TASH: Decorating. Got a mate decorating. A mate's bloke. she's pregnant. Very nearly due.

SQUEAL: Great.

TASH: They were planning but they weren't planning then bam –

SQUEAL: It's not as hard as it looks.

TASH: No. (*Going.*) I'm decorating. I've got a mate decorating. My mate's bloke. He's –

SQUEAL: Great.

TASH: That's your favourite word.

SQUEAL: A man of few.

TASH: Okay then. Bye.

TASH makes to go.

SQUEAL: Is that it? 'Okay then. Bye.'

TASH: I'm going for mauve on the kitchen walls and yellow in the bedroom. I know purple's a bit ecclesiastical but fuck it, it's a nice colour, it's a calming colour.

SQUEAL: What are you talking about Tash?

TASH: I thought you wanted to talk a bit longer.

SQUEAL: Why are you so weird? Why can't you just do simple things normal?

TASH: I'm talking.

SQUEAL: You're being all weird.

TASH: Weird like what?

SQUEAL: Weird like this. I only asked you for a cup of coffee. It's okay, you don't have to say yes. I'm not breaking my heart over it.

TASH: Fine. Okay. Nice seeing you then.

SQUEAL: Tash.

TASH: Do you know that a woman was standing on a golf course in Berkshire and it was raining so hard that a small koi carp with an ID tag clipped on its fin fell from the sky? It had got vacummed up in the big weather cycle in Tokyo. I read that in the paper this morning.

SQUEAL: (*Laughing.*) You're amazing.

TASH: At least I'm making conversation. I'm talking, saying something instead of 'Yeah great.'

SQUEAL: Okay.

TASH: It's hardly fighting the chemistry. You could hardly say that you and I talk and we're fighting the chemistry.

SQUEAL: Slow down, slow down.

TASH: You get good value for money with me.

SQUEAL: I never said –

TASH: If you want to talk to one of those daft bitches who simper at your every word, then go fling around your 'greats' and 'yeah okay' somewhere else.

SQUEAL: Fine, cheers, enough said. Have a nice day.

TASH: Don't look injured.

SQUEAL: Look what?

TASH: If you can't do it, don't stop me in the street and say hello. I've passed you twice this week –

SQUEAL: I didn't see you –

TASH: – on the bus and you've said fuck all.

Silence.

SQUEAL: On the bus?

Silence. TASH and SQUEAL start to laugh.

How was I meant to see you if you were sitting on a bloody bus?

Silence.

TASH: Goodbye then.

SQUEAL: We could go and have a coffee.

TASH: No thanks.

SQUEAL: (*Calling after.*) Tash… Tash… Can I have your phone number?

TASH: What? And never fucking call?

TASH exits. SQUEAL looks on. Rain.

Scene 10

Flat, London. AL scraping paper off the walls with long smooth moves. TASH standing, eating back of the fridge food.

AL: China and Malaysia. There's a few left in India, but to be honest the indigenous Tiger, I reckon there's probably not more than 100 – 150 left in the world.

TASH: Right.

AL: That doesn't include breeds in captivity. There's a small ratio of the rarer breeds that are surviving solely on the fact that there are a quantity of them still bred in captivity. Like the Siberian White Tiger which I reckon there aren't more than 30 – 35 alive in the wild.

TASH: Yeah.

AL: Remember I adopted one for Hen's brother last Christmas. Whipsnade do them.

TASH: Yeah. I remember her saying.

AL: You'll get indigestion eating like that.

TASH: It's the way I always eat.

AL: If you folded out that table you could move my brushes over a bit and sit down.

TASH: I like standing up. I'm going out later.

AL: My dad got a hernia always eating standing up on the job – Conductor.

TASH: Yeah, Al. I know. You say it everytime you come around and I'm standing eating like this.

AL: Mind my own. Sorry. These are good walls underneath here.

TASH: Yeah, what's Hen doing tonight?

AL: Watching telly. I'll get us a takeway later.

TASH: Friday night and you're staying in?

AL: Yeah.

TASH: Friday night and you're staying in?

AL: We got a parrot in here? We can't do much at the moment. Hen's knackered.

TASH: She shouldn't be working.

AL: I keep telling her.

TASH: Do you?

AL: Yeah. What you looking at me like that for?

TASH: How long have you been with Hen?

AL: '94, '95 – Six years.

TASH: Long time.

AL: Life time. For me. I couldn't get a girlfriend before her.

TASH: Really?

AL: Ha ha. (*Pointing to ceiling.*) You want me to do that bit as well?

TASH nods.

Hen keeps saying, when are you going to settle?

TASH: No. You all have a perverse interest in understanding why I'm not doing what you're all doing. I think you're worried I know something you don't. I don't mind. My family have long stopped minding. This is it. This is me.

AL: Nice cornicing.

TASH: I love you.

AL: I don't make her work. I'd prefer it if she didn't work.

TASH: You need the money, she says.

AL: We'd manage.

TASH: Doing up your house is like haemorrhaging money.

AL: It's a good investment.

TASH: You've been stung.

AL: Bollocks, you don't know what you're talking about.

TASH: I saw you.

AL: What? I can scrape off the paint around the moulding that will clean it up a bit.

TASH: I saw you. How old is she? Sixteen? Seventeen?

AL: I don't know what you're talking about.

TASH: Boss' daughter? Work placement?

AL: (*Laughing.*) You can't be serious. I'm not taking it serious. You are being serious. How long have I been with Hen? How long have you known me?

TASH: You're still a bloke.

AL stops work, laughing.

AL: You're serious.

TASH makes to go.

TASH: You're insulted.

AL: Too fucking right I'm insulted. A sixteen year old temp. Not finished her A levels. You don't get it do you? You sad, silly cow, you don't get it.

TASH: I'm just saying. I know. I'm just saying I know. So do something about it.

AL: (*Beat.*) What were we doing? On this hot date? What were we doing?

TASH: You were buying sandwiches. You were having a sandwich.

AL: Bloody hell. Ham or egg?

TASH: Don't piss around.

AL: You don't piss around. You don't fucking piss around. Tash. Are you honestly serious?

TASH: You touched her arm. You were holding her by the arm. Sort it out or I'm telling Hen.

AL: Telling her what? (*Beat.*) Telling her what?

TASH: Don't make me say it.

AL: You don't know what you're fucking talking about.

Silence

When was the last time you were touched eh? Can you remember? And I don't mean some drunk grope in the back of a cab. When was the last time? I'll tell you when I was. This morning, just as I was going out, I reached for my keys and Hen brushed the back of my neck. She leant back, from reading her visa bill and she stroked the back of my neck. I've had six years of that and I still like it. And you think I'd give that up for some tossy little feel over a mozzarella and avocado ciabatta.

Silence

You should get out more.

TASH: (*Beat.*) Too much keeping me up at night.

AL: Like you're proud of it. Like picking men up in the way you do is something to brag about…

TASH: I hinted. There was no bragging involved.

AL: So why tell Hen all about it all the time? (*Beat.*) It hurts her.

TASH: Maybe I'm having a better time.

AL: She loves you.

TASH holds AL's stare.

TASH: You haven't got the monopoly on that. (*Beat.*) Do something.

AL: Six years? You think I'm about to throw away six years?

AL returns to scraping the walls. TASH carries on eating, watching him.

I don't know what you're talking about.

Scene 11

Supermarket, South London. SQUEAL is standing talking to NATHAN who is videoing him as he takes things off shelves and puts them into his basket.

NATHAN: And coffee is how you start your day?

SQUEAL: Yeah. I suppose so. Yeah, coffee is what I normally have. Does the shop pay you to do this?

NATHAN: It's client based. If you could just turn the lid a little, so I could catch the label. Logo registering.

SQUEAL: I don't really believe in this.

NATHAN: It's helping people. It's helping us help people decide what they need to buy.

SQUEAL: What they *need* to buy? What you want them to buy?

NATHAN: And after the coffee?

SQUEAL: I'm sure you have to do your job but I've just come in for a jar of coffee maybe some biscuits for later not to help your fat cat boss shove us more junk we don't need, okay?

NATHAN: Yeah, I completely understand it's just your input would be invaluable. I just have two more people to do and then I can finish for the day.

SQUEAL: It's only half past eight.

NATHAN: I started early. I was let down.

SQUEAL: And I do night shifts so if you wouldn't mind.

A man (MARVIN) shuffles past, a pint of milk in hand, browsing over tea bags. SQUEAL resumes his search for the biscuits.

NATHAN: (*To MARVIN.*) This is the tea and coffee section, don't let me disturb your normal pattern of behaviour but was that actually the teabags you were looking for?

MARVIN: It's whatever's the cheapest.

NATHAN: Interesting. Very interesting. You work?

MARVIN: Sorry.

NATHAN: You do something in the service industry.

MARVIN: Sorry.

NATHAN: We find a high percentage of the technical professions or even service industry tend to favour that brand of particular beverage.

SQUEAL: The guy is just buying tea. Could you not go and do this somewhere else?

NATHAN: You see I'd like to be able to say yes but this is highly important, highly sensitive information.

MARVIN: I work in the cleaning industry. I like to bring my own tea.

NATHAN: Right. So I wasn't that far left of field. Very interesting. Very kind of you to divulge. Share.

SQUEAL shakes his head as he makes to go.

You will be having milk with that coffee?

SQUEAL: Possibly.

NATHAN: Natural or freeze dried? (*Beat.*) Coffee mate or cow's own?

SQUEAL: Are you taking the piss?

MARVIN: Excuse me, do you know where they've moved the detergents?

SQUEAL: Sorry?

MARVIN moves off. SQUEAL continues with his shopping. NATHAN films throughout.

SQUEAL: Could you stop that now please? Please? (*To checkout girl.*) Could you tell him to stop or I'll call the manager? Please. It's been a long night. I've been on the night shift. Please.

NATHAN refuses to stop as he films the contents of the shopping bag.

NATHAN: Almost finished.

MARVIN: I think you should perhaps leave the gentleman alone.

NATHAN: It's important for the advertising…

SQUEAL: You should know better. You should know better not to tell people to drink more, to eat more, to live more, to buy more. Do you know what people like you do? The damage that people like you do. I see the damage that people like you create. The stress in people's lives to buy more, to keep up the mortgage repayments, to have another drink to eleviate that stress, to eat another fat filled pile of crap which clogs up the heart and make it difficult to live, to even breath. I've just spent last night working on the heart of a very fat man, opening it up and discovering the consequences of what you sell. The pain that you deliver. The hope that you give people, to make their lives better, for more, more, more.

SQUEAL, through his tirade, has managed to push the man up against the wall of the supermarket as MARVIN looks on.

What happened to love and care and not thinking that *you* know what people *need?* When they don't even know themselves.

MARVIN: Alright, son. Calm down? Okay?

SQUEAL slowly eases his grip, nodding. Then holding up the bottle of coffee he shows the label to the camera.

NATHAN: I'm sorry. I'm really very sorry.

SQUEAL turns and puts down his coffee and exits. MARVIN takes in the scene.

MARVIN: You alright?

NATHAN nods.

If he'd thumped, you could have sued.

NATHAN nods, clearly shaken as MARVIN resumes his shopping.

NATHAN: Would you mind if I filmed you doing that?

MARVIN shakes his head and shuffles away, with NATHAN following him.

It would help if we start with your name.

MARVIN: (*Long beat.*) Marvin.

MARVIN turns and hesitates, staring at first NATHAN and then the camera.

I know you. I clean in your block.

NATHAN: Do you?

MARVIN: I do all the blocks around there.

NATHAN: Marvin.

MARVIN: (*Beat.*) I'm looking for the polish but they've moved it all around so – I'm lost.

NATHAN: (*Without looking up from camera.*) And now you are found.

INTERVAL

Scene 12

Surburban garden, East London. GLORIA is hanging out washing. HEN is standing talking to her. GLORIA keeps coming to a man's shirt at the bottom of the pile and stopping herself, shuffling through the wet washing for anything but –

GLORIA: You don't normally. It's not normal for you to visit at home.

Silence.

HEN: We had an anonymous call last week. A possible sighting. It's the normal feedback when we've done any recent press release.People want to help but this time, I have to say the description was surprisingly accurate.

GLORIA stands frozen to the spot.

It's several hundred miles from here but it could be…

GLORIA: Do you know the American backstroke is different from the English?

HEN shakes her head. GLORIA puts down her washing and demonstrates, kicking with one arm and a leg.

It's a sharp straight down movement, so you slice the water. I've been learning them both and it definitely improves your speed, not that I am concerned about speed but it is nice to know one has the option.

HEN nods. GLORIA smiles. She takes the washing inside. HEN shifts her hand suddenly across her bump. She felt something kick.

HEN: I'm sure he doesn't think that.

GLORIA: How do you know?

HEN: Those who are left often blame themselves.

GLORIA: And those who leave should stop and think what they're bloody doing. (*Beat.*) Shouldn't they?

HEN: Do you want to follow up that sighting. It is quite a way away but –

GLORIA: How far?

HEN: Skye. Just off the coast of Skye.

Silence.

I've an address. If you'll take it. Or I can arrange for someone to perhaps go with you if you don't want to go on your own.

Silence.

No one is forcing you.

Silence.

There's no guarantee. I don't want to raise your hopes.

GLORIA: But anything is better than nothing?

GLORIA pauses, looking down into the washing basket. She is down to the last shirt.

I don't miss his nail clippings in the bath, coat never hung up, channel flicking, he always was channel flicking just when you were settling down, enjoying something. The way he ate, he was a noisy eater, a little click, his jaw clicked, clicked so I knew he was sat at the table before I'd even put the plates down. I don't miss his silence and his little observations, the birds, we've got a lot of birds in the garden… 'Look, Gloria, isn't that a…' I don't know. I don't know. 'The blue one, the little blue one with the yellow tip, look it up in the book…' Always reading too late at night, reading me bits, letting me fall asleep while he was reading me bits. And always being too hot, always too hot in bed, getting up to get water in the night and waking me… 'Sweetheart, have a sip. You don't drink enough.' I don't. He's right, I don't.

HEN: If it is him?

GLORIA: You ever sit in silence with someone so long…that only the fart behind his newspaper breaks it…makes you laugh. The way he used to do that. Always use to do that. All those little things.

Silence.

I guess that's married life for you.

HEN: (*Beat.*) I'm not married.

GLORIA: Who is now? Kids, and love and electric bills aren't really that important. What's holding us together is very fragile indeed.

HEN: Kids, and love and electric bills *are* everything.

GLORIA laughs.

GLORIA: Everything and nothing.

HEN: What else are you doing with someone? If that's not it –

Silence.

GLORIA: You're having a baby. We never had children. How can I say – We never had children. I'm sorry.

HEN: It's fine.

GLORIA: What would I know?

Silence.

HEN: This wasn't planned.

Silence.

Al, my boyfriend…he calls it a random event. He hates the idea of any kind of destiny. I find it hurtful. It wakes me in the night the thought that if this is random it could have been anybody's but for that one night it was me. That this could be someone else. He thinks I'm talking about destiny but I'm not. I'm talking about the fact that in meeting me there was nobody else. In meeting me I was the only mother possible for his child.

GLORIA: There's always somebody else.

Silence.

HEN: I don't want to hear that. I'm sorry. I hear you now but I don't want to. I'm sorry. I'm sorry.

GLORIA finally pins up the man's shirt. HEN clocks it.

GLORIA: There's always one that sneaks into the washing somehow.

Silence.

HEN: Let's talk about…

GLORIA: Scotland.

Silence.

HEN: Good. (*Beat.*) It should be beautiful this time of the year.

Scene 13

Flat, London. MARVIN cleaning NATHAN's flat; bin bag, duster, polish. An oil lamp. MARVIN flicks it on and waits. The bubble of oil doesn't move. NATHAN comes through reading some papers.

NATHAN: It needs to heat up. The oil? It won't do anything until it's had time to get hot, to soften.

MARVIN nods. Returns to work. Dusting.

You okay?

MARVIN: Bin bags.

NATHAN: Top drawer.

MARVIN shakes out a bin bag.

You found them.

MARVIN: You need some more. I've put them on your list.

NATHAN: Thank you. You're finding everything okay?

MARVIN: I have a room at the hostel. Suits me fine. I can keep the same bed. If you pay in the morning you can keep the same bed.

NATHAN: And that's…

MARVIN: Suits me fine. I can keep the same bed. If you pay in the morning you keep the same bed.

NATHAN: That must be comforting.

MARVIN: That's all I need.

NATHAN: Yes.

MARVIN: You're not working…

NATHAN: Not today. (*Long beat.*) I won't get in your way.

MARVIN: That's fine. I was wondering about the ladies things in the cupboard.

NATHAN: Yes –

MARVIN: It's just, they're taking up a lot of room, and I was wondering if you wanted me to move them down to the bigger one in the hall.

NATHAN: No.

MARVIN: (*Long beat.*) I won't bother hoovering today.

NATHAN: Thank you.

MARVIN: You need more polish as well.

NATHAN: You put it?

MARVIN: On the list.

NATHAN: Thank you.

Silence.

Marvin, you didn't always –

MARVIN: No… I've always been in cleaning of some kind but –

NATHAN: I thought not. I was thinking how's someone like him ended up –

MARVIN: I've been on a kind of holiday. Still on it really it. This is my time out time. You should try it. Some time out time.

NATHAN: Yes.

MARVIN: Gives you a perspective.

NATHAN: (*Beat.*) Some things you can never get a perspective on.

MARVIN: Then you take time out until you do – (*Sniffing duster.*) Nice smell. There's nothing…there's nothing like a woman's perfume. I was just dusting some of those cupboards. It lingers.

NATHAN: There's a married man talking.

Silence.

My wife left – a while ago.

MARVIN: When you tell me that, I feel…

NATHAN: It's really very common.

MARVIN: That I understand you. That I understand what you must be going through. You didn't have…

NATHAN: Not having children makes it easier.

MARVIN: Not having children makes it possible. She wouldn't have left if you'd had children.

NATHAN: You think?

MARVIN: A child is innocent. A child is something small. Always, even when they are big, to you, a parent, they are always small. She wouldn't have left her child. That would be too much to ask you to bear.

NATHAN: Whatever.

MARVIN: It gets lonely.

Silence.

NATHAN: Opposite, you see there, the one with the blinds. There is a woman. I see her in the supermarket. She buys meals for two, enough for two people, but it's just her. I never see her with anyone. (*Looking out of window.*) Those windows out there become my friends. Those inroads into other people's lives. You must find that. As a cleaner. You are given a root in, to see the way other people live.

The lady who buys her meals for two buys so much because she has an elderly neighbour who can't get out herself. She divides everything she buys by two and shares it with her. I do the stairs outside her landing Tuesdays and Thursdays. The man, who you think is divorced, is not divorced. He is happily married but has chosen not to live with his wife, he spends every Sunday with her. I clean on Sundays when he is out. You see there are alternative ways of living, alternative families.

NATHAN: That's very reassuring.

MARVIN: Don't be cynical.

NATHAN: I'm not. I find that really very reassuring. People can be disappointing. Only the other week I was let down.

MARVIN: Right.

NATHAN: I had to cover for someone at work. (*Beat.*) Which was inconvenient.

MARVIN: (*Beat.*) Would you like me to do your bedroom now?

NATHAN: Yes. And in the afternoon…

MARVIN: In the afternoon?

NATHAN: I may go out.

MARVIN: And later?

NATHAN: I won't need you later.

MARVIN: I can go back to the hostel then. I don't like to be late. You can get tea between five to seven p.m.

NATHAN: That must be…

MARVIN: It's convenient. That's when I like to eat.

NATHAN: And what do you do in the evenings.

MARVIN: Sometimes I just lie on my bed and think. Or I sit at the window and listen to the different noises. Someone laughing or a shout down the corridor. And I try and work out what's happened. I set the scene in my head. The moment before, the minutes after. Or I just watch the flies zig zagging around the shade above. They move in a very definate way. Zig zag…zig zag… They leave an imaginary line, almost visible, they move so fast. Sometimes one of the other blokes, there are only men in our dormitory, sometimes one of them will go and cry out in the night and I'll go and sit at the end of whoever's bed, and share a fag, or talk, or just sometimes I just sit, even lie next to them, hold their hand, great big men holding hands, I never thought I'd see it, not like you think, just giving people company, being almost tender and I stay with them until the morning. They've normally pissed the bed or are shouting for a drink, whatever wakes me up first – The wet through the trousers or the great whisky breath on my neck.

NATHAN: (*Long beat.*) Are you happy?

MARVIN: …I don't think I've ever been happier in my life.

Scene 14

Restaurant, London. SQUEAL, TASH, HEN and AL are midway through dinner. Chinese. Flock wallpaper. Shanghai Lil music.

AL: Amputation. That's hardcore.

SQUEAL: It's just one part of the surgery I do.

AL: Wow. What do people normally have –

SQUEAL: Mainly limbs.

TASH: Please.

HEN: Please.

SQUEAL: I'm mainly casualty. Dog biscuits up the nose, that kind of stuff –

AL: Hoovers stuck up peoples arses.

HEN: Al. Stop talking like –

TASH: – a builder.

AL: (*To SQUEAL.*) She's a horror. You realise she's a horror. I have to work around her everyday.

TASH: Not everyday.

AL: She doesn't get out of bed.

TASH: This is not true. I get out of bed to make you tea and sandwiches?

HEN: You sound like an old married couple…

A ripple of laughter.

AL: You should get out more.

HEN: Why don't you go on holiday?

TASH: Maybe

HEN: Kick start things a bit again for you.

TASH: I don't think we need to talk about this now. It's not your mission to get my life back on track.

SQUEAL: I don't mind.

HEN: Have you travelled?

SQUEAL: I did a year overseas as part of my medical training. Australia. Perth.

AL: I'd love to go to Australia. Did you know the indigenous Wallaby outnumbers the domestic dog by forty to one in the outback?

TASH: (*To SQUEAL.*) National Geographic. The Holy Grail.

HEN: I didn't know that. I didn't know you wanted to go to Australia.

AL: Yeah, you did. I'm always saying I'd love to travel.

HEN: I can't even get him to go out of London for a weekend and he's talking about Australia.

AL: That's proper travel. That's not like a weekend in Tenby. I'd like to do a lot of South East Asia as well. Malaysia, China… I've got a mate who's working on some apartments in Singapore.

SQUEAL: Singapore's fantastic. I spent a month there.

HEN: You never said this. You've never mentioned this before.

AL: I have. I've always said I'd like to travel. Maybe do India. I've always wanted to go to India.

SQUEAL: If you're doing India, you've got to head south. Sri Lanka.

AL: Yeah.

SQUEAL: It's an amazing country. I mean really amazing. I mean I'm not talking about all the tourism and the sleazy end of it but if you really spend some time there. It's Buddhist and yet there's a lot of Catholicism so you've got these two faiths side by side. You can be driving down the road and on one side you've got these fantastic Buddhist Temples, I mean really ornate and yet go in them and its so humble, so peaceful. I mean I'm not religious, but there you start to believe in something beyond this, something linking us all then on the other side you've got all hell and damnation and then you start looking at the Buddhist temples again and you realise it's all just the same thing. They've got devils and demons and crocodiles eating elephants and its just everyone trying to believe in something beyond themselves. Know what I mean?

AL: Yeah. Yeah. And somewhere, I don't know where it is, there's this, there's this waterfall that falls down into this inland pool that's so deep that no one has ever actually got to the bottom and you can go there and stay days because all around the edges are these tiny caves and you build fires and sleep by the water at night and in the day you can do this trek to the top of the waterfall and people do these river jumps and they say if you do touch the bottom you've been touched by the hand of God and that if you survive it – you grow a third leg that turns into a fin over night.

AL starts laughing.

TASH: Funny. Very funny. Did anyone get that down?

AL: Sorry…mate… Sorry.

TASH: (*To AL.*) You're an arse.

SQUEAL: You're alright.

HEN: It sounds beautiful. It sounds amazing.

SQUEAL: It is.

HEN: (*Beat.*) We should go then.

SQUEAL: I've got some books on it if you want to have a look.

AL: It might be a bit hard with the baby.

TASH: You can do anything with a baby. I bet there were people out there with babies. Life goes on with a baby.

AL: It would with you, yeah. But then life goes on with whatever, doesn't it Tash? No job, you just get another, no bloke just pick up another fuck for the night.

HEN: Al –

AL: You do know she's incapable of sustaining anything she won't be able to rip down and replaster next week.

TASH: I'm not listening.

AL: When was the last time anyone said they'd loved you, Tash?

TASH: What's this turnaround?

AL: When?

TASH: You'll be the first to know.

AL: Not yet then. Point proven. Incapable.

TASH: That really is straight to the nuts even for you.

AL: It's what people say to each other.

HEN: Give it a rest, Al.

AL: It's what people feel for each other –

Silence.

When?

Silence.

When?

Silence.

SQUEAL: I love her.

   Silence.

TASH: You hardly know me.

SQUEAL: I wasn't saying marrry me.

TASH: Don't give me the sympathy vote.

HEN: Tash –

TASH: You love me. Is that what you think I need? You think that does the trick? I'm not a charity.

SQUEAL: I didn't do that for a good cause.

TASH: Why did you then?

   Silence.

   I wasn't incarcerated and I wasn't abused. I have very nice parents and a brother with three kids. He's normal, too normal some might say. I have a healthy appetite, I don't get into abusive relationships, I don't get into relationships, I wasn't bullied and I had a fantastic time at college, careers a bit shaky but fuck it I've still got my own teeth, so the last thing I need –

SQUEAL: Forget it.

TASH: You're the one who's embarrassed yourself.

   Silence. TASH exits. SQUEAL, AL and HEN sit in silence.

HEN: (*Beat.*) You never said you wanted to travel.

AL: Someone was just talking about it at work.

HEN: Someone?

Silence. HEN scrapes her chair back and exits. AL and SQUEAL sit in silence until –

SQUEAL: Shall I get the bill?

Scene 15

Flat, London. Morning. NATHAN is making breakfast. Coffee, bagels, cream cheese. Sound of a shower turning off. NATHAN waits until – TASH comes through in a towel.

NATHAN: You found –

TASH: Yeah.

NATHAN nods, pours TASH a cup of coffee. TASH picks up a shoe.

One more to go.

NATHAN: I've got bagels.

TASH: (*Beat.*) Great.

TASH exits. NATHAN starts to toast bagels, read the paper, flick around with the radio until – TASH comes back through, now half dressed, pulling on her shirt, the same clothes from the night before. NATHAN slides her over a cup of coffee.

Thanks. I'm sorry… I'm sorry I didn't show last week.

NATHAN: I had to cover –

TASH: Yeah.

NATHAN: I had to cover for you.

TASH: Yeah. I'm sorry.

NATHAN: It's probably, it's probably a sackable offence.

TASH laughs. NATHAN laughs. NATHAN goes to talk to her. TASH moves away.

TASH: Nice coffee.

NATHAN: Yeah.

TASH: Good.

NATHAN: Bagel.

TASH: Great.

TASH doesn't touch her breakfast.

I don't normally eat breakfast.

NATHAN: Right. Okay. Don't worry. Would you like cereal?

TASH: No, coffee's great.

Silence. TASH drinks, unsure what to do next.

I used some of your shampoo and a toothbrush as well.

NATHAN: Mia casa your casa.

Silence.

TASH: I might get a move on then.

NATHAN: Now.

TASH: Yeah.

NATHAN: I thought we could –

TASH: No. Sorry.

NATHAN: It's just last night –

TASH: I didn't want to go home.

NATHAN: I thought we could spend the day together.

TASH: Please. I know where this is going – I'm sorry but that's not the way it works. Why don't people get that? I don't know why you like me. Is it because I'm here? You seem like a very nice guy. A very nice lonely guy.

NATHAN: No.

TASH: Who thinks that I'm the answer. But I'm not…

Silence.

NATHAN: Right.

Silence.

TASH: I was lonely. I was lonely too last night.

Silence.

You live close.

NATHAN: Of course. Sure. Of course.

TASH: I feel a shit now.

NATHAN: Don't –

Silence.

Why should you feel bad? We both got what we want.

TASH: Not exactly.

NATHAN: So shall we say Monday?

TASH: You serious?

NATHAN: You want a job don't you?

Silence. TASH nods.

TASH: I used the hairbrush as well. There were a lot of blonde hairs and I'm dark so if she sees, whoever she is, can you apologise –

Silence.

I wasn't really looking for anything more than –

NATHAN: Someone to lie with.

TASH: Yeah. (*Beat.*) So it didn't matter.

Silence.

Everyone has that problem once in a while.

NATHAN: Not me. I bring girls back all the time.

TASH: Yeah.

NATHAN: Yeah. So really it made a change.

TASH: I should go.

NATHAN: Yeah.

TASH wavers at the door. Silence.

TASH: I was out for supper last night. With a friend, my best friend and her boyfriend and we got into this sort of fight and I was with another friend and we were coming home and suddenly I just couldn't be on my own. I couldn't think where else to go.

NATHAN: (*Beat.*) Sure.

TASH nods.

TASH: See you Monday.

TASH makes to go.

NATHAN: Looking forward to it. (*Beat.*) You know you really are quite a cunt.

TASH hesitates, exits. NATHAN sits on his own. He stares down at the second cup of coffee and bagel. He suddenly gets up, scoops up plates, bagel, cup in one move and shoves it in the sink.

Scene 16

Bed and Breakfast, Scotland. GLORIA is standing brushing her teeth. She is talking to herself.

GLORIA: Not today. Please not today. Yesterday, when I needed you, where were you? Not today. I was walking and I was looking for you everywhere. Do you know how many pubs there are? Sitting on my own in a pub, hoping – Marvin? And I had this thought, it crossed my mind, it was more a feeling, a very strong sensation, that when you're in my mind, every moment that I'm thinking of you, every blinding, boring moment, that I'm carrying you close to me, talking to you, wanting you…you want no one. Not me No one. You need no one. I feel sick. I want to vomit. I want to –

GLORIA looks at herself in the mirror, as she waits in expectation of some kind of response. She breathes heavy against the mirror.

Skye.

The squawk of gulls outside, making her turn and look out for a moment. She returns to cleaning her teeth, finishes, picks up a towel, her costume, contemplates with terror.

Come back. Come back. I don't know how much longer –

The lap of sea water.

Scene 17

Bar, London. TASH and HEN sitting perched, drinking. Noise all around.

TASH: Forget it.

HEN: No, it was horrible of him.

TASH: I've know him too long. I've known you both too long. It was fine.

HEN: I felt terrible.

TASH: Friends, good friends have those kind of…scuffles.

HEN: He's cooking tonight.

TASH: He said. I saw the…

HEN: Curry. He always cooks curry.

TASH: And you always hate it. Why don't you say to him?

HEN: Too late. Should have done it years ago but now… I've been eating it and telling him I love it. We've bonded over that curry. We've made babies over that curry. (*Beat.*) You saw Al today –

TASH: (*Beat.*) He's almost finished the bathroom.

HEN: Well when he's finished with yours ask if he can knock ours on the head, eh? I don't know if we're ever going to get into that house.

TASH: You can have him back anytime you want.

HEN: Has it made it difficult?

TASH: It's fine. We both ignored it… It was ignored the next day. (*Beat.*) He had a point.

HEN: He cares about you. (*Beat.*) He cares about me, therefore he cares about you. (*Beat.*) He does.

TASH: Are you feeling – ?

HEN: Great… Fat… Fat and ugly…

TASH: No…

HEN: Yes.

TASH: This is when you say… 'He doesn't want to sleep with me anymore.'

HEN: (*Beat.*) He doesn't want to sleep with me anymore. (*Beat.*) Not.

A ripple of laughter.

Have you seen –

TASH: This bar is really noisy.

HEN: Deflection.

TASH: Overturned. I don't want to talk about –

HEN: I didn't say anything.

TASH: I don't want to talk about him. Do you need some kind of reassurance? Am I some kind of loose cannon like you want to partner me up?

HEN: It's okay… It's okay…

TASH: Why do you always say that? 'It's okay…it's okay…'

HEN: Sorry…

TASH: Stop it will you…

HEN: What?

TASH: Please, fight back a bit Hen –

HEN: This is not important enough. We've had a good evening. Why are you spoiling it now? You've had a bad day? I'm sorry if you've had a bad day.

TASH: I've not had a bad day… Stop accommodating me…

HEN: What, have I done? I don't get it… This is what I do… I listen… You talk…

TASH: I know.

HEN: Is there something you're not telling me?

TASH: No…

HEN: Tash…

TASH: Just back off Hen. Your life's okay, alright?

HEN: I never said it wasn't. *I* never said it wasn't. Is Al sleeping with someone?

TASH: You're so fucking dramatic.

HEN: I'd rather know.

TASH: I was talking about me –

HEN: Is that why you brought me here?

TASH: No. Hen? (*Long beat.*) No… He loves you.

HEN: How do you know?

TASH: He does. Where's all this come from?

Silence.

He does.

Silence.

HEN: Liar.

HEN orders another drink.

Scene 18

Flat, London. MARVIN entering the flat, pausing on seeing –

NATHAN: (*Calling out.*) Marvin –

A row of woman's clothes, dresses etc., hanging up, in bags as if ready to be thrown out as NATHAN comes through carrying more dresses on hangers.

If there's anything you would like take it.

NATHAN exits. MARVIN goes over and touches the dresses as NATHAN comes through carrying boxes of shoes.

Obviously that's not your colour but I thought maybe people at the hostel.

MARVIN: It's all men.

NATHAN: (*Beat.*) There's some good coats.

NATHAN exits. MARVIN opens one of the boxes, takes out a shoe as NATHAN comes back through, two big bin bags in hand.

I think it's a waste leaving them kicking around in the back of a cupboard when somebody could be getting pleasure out of them.

MARVIN: Right.

NATHAN: I could drive you to the charity shops if you don't want them.

MARVIN: That might be an idea.

NATHAN: We could pick up some supper after.

MARVIN: I have to be back at the hostel.

NATHAN: Let your hair down for a night, Marvin. When was the last time you went to a restaurant?

MARVIN: I go to Starbucks most days.

NATHAN: I want to take you out.

NATHAN exits.

MARVIN: (*Calling out.*) Oxfam is the nearest.

As NATHAN comes back through with the last bag.

NATHAN: Whatever.

Clocking MARVIN watching him.

You're always telling me to clear out that cupboard.

MARVIN nods, he looks at the shoe in his hand.

MARVIN: These are beautiful.

NATHAN: They've already dated. They're fashionable so I suppose they date quicker.

MARVIN: They're still beautiful.

MARVIN looks at the tiny straps of the shoe.

You forget how thin a woman's ankle is.

NATHAN: Yes.

MARVIN nods, carefully puts the shoe back.

MARVIN: My wife liked –

Silence.

I'll clean out that room then.

NATHAN nods. MARVIN makes to go, pulling off his coat.

NATHAN: And after we'll go out and eat.

MARVIN: I have to be back at the hostel before eight.

NATHAN: They don't lock you in. You can come and go, surely.

MARVIN: I like the routine.

NATHAN: For one night –

Silence.

MARVIN: I'll say no. But thank you.

Silence. MARVIN makes to go.

NATHAN: Marvin, I want you to come out to supper tonight. You've been a very good friend to me these last few weeks. Steak. You like steak I bet.

MARVIN: I don't eat meat much now.

NATHAN: Well tonight –

MARVIN: I don't really like going out. I've found a life that suits me. I don't mean to be rude, Nathan. You're a good boy but –

NATHAN: Say yes. Please say fucking yes Marvin. Say yes.

MARVIN: I'm your cleaner.

NATHAN: You're saying no.

MARVIN: I prefer to – I prefer just to work if you don't mind.

NATHAN: I'll pay you. How much do you cost for a night? Just for the company.

MARVIN: You must have friends. A man like you must have –

NATHAN: I want someone I don't know. I want a friend I don't know. Tell me about yourself Marvin. Your wife?

MARVIN: I'll clean the back room.

NATHAN: Twenty – twenty-five, I'll give you twenty-five quid. (*Beat.*) We could go to the cashpoint.

NATHAN starts trying to shove money into MARVIN's hand. MARVIN stands embarrassed.

MARVIN: Please –

NATHAN: I just want someone to have a fucking pizza with –

Silence.

It was just an idea.

MARVIN: A nice idea.

Silence.

Why don't you get one of your lady friends to take you out?

Silence.

I wouldn't be able to pay.

NATHAN shrugs.

Nathan, have you thought of going to talk to someone?

NATHAN half laughs to himself.

MARVIN: I'll clean the bathroom while I'm at it.

NATHAN nods.

NATHAN: I don't understand you. I don't understand people.

Silence.

I'll get changed then. I'm starving.

NATHAN exits. MARVIN is left standing looking at all the clothes. He goes to touch them and them stops himself.

Scene 19

Bedroom, London. HEN and AL are lying in bed.

HEN: We don't do this –

AL: No.

HEN: We don't do this enough. Like being on holiday.

AL: A one hour holiday.

HEN: A lunch hour holiday. (*Sudden start.*) Did you feel it move?

AL: What?

HEN: It moved. More than a nudge, a real kick.

AL: I felt nothing.

HEN: Wait. (*Long wait.*) Feel?

AL: No, nothing.

HEN: Never mind.

AL: Footballer. It's definitely going to be a footballer.

HEN: Yes. (*Long beat.*) Have you talked to Tash yet?

AL: No.

HEN: You ought to say sorry.

AL: No.

HEN: It was cruel what you said.

AL: It was true.

HEN: She hasn't rung all week.

AL: Enjoy the peace.

HEN: Blokes never get, they never get girlfriends.

AL: I have mates.

HEN: Yeah but not like girlfriends. (*Beat.*) This is nice.

AL: Uh huh.

HEN: It's just…

AL: Something on your mind…

HEN: Someone finishing my sentences before I ever get to the end of them. Sorry. Sorry.

AL: (*Jumping up.*) Jesus… That was a Beckham punch. I felt it…

HEN: Did you?

AL: Right in the face. Really big boot right in the chops.

HEN: See. That's what I'm living with. That's what I'm waking up with.

AL: Uh huh…

HEN: To find you're not home… (*Long silence.*) Where were you Thursday night?

AL: Home.

HEN: No, you weren't. I woke up. I woke up at three and you weren't even back.

AL: It was eleven. You'd just gone to sleep. I promise you.

HEN: And I felt a kick in my stomach and I opened my eyes thinking it was you but you weren't home. So I waited up and when you did creep in at 4.30… I'd closed my eyes and pretended I was asleep, with it still kicking me, with me wanting to scream out and you just lay there with your eyes open, not moving…

AL: No…

HEN: And you're face smelt. You hadn't even bothered to wash your face.

AL: Hen… This is mad…

HEN: Tell me then different. Tell me different…

AL: I don't know what you're talking about.

HEN: I do… I do…

Scene 20

Office, London. GLORIA sits tapping details into a computer. NATHAN sits opposite. He shifts in his chair, as if short of time.

GLORIA: A natural blonde. That's very rare now.

NATHAN: I thought she was but after… When she'd gone, I discovered the hair bleach… She dyed it, and yet she'd always told me that it was her own natural colour.

GLORIA: A white lie. Husbands and wives need little white lies.

NATHAN: She was a very honest person. She was a very straight person.

GLORIA: It's a nice name.

NATHAN: It still has a kind of magic for me. I find it disturbing when I meet other people who have the same name. A lot of faces. (*Pointing.*) On the walls. A lot of people missing.

GLORIA: Yes. But they are found. Many of them, the majority of them are eventually traced. Do you have a job?

NATHAN: Yes… I'm freelance now… I work when I feel like it.

GLORIA: Who for?

NATHAN: Myself… People. I have been recording people. On film. Notating them down. Their habits.

GLORIA: For?

NATHAN: Clients.

GLORIA: You're an academic.

NATHAN: Yes… It's a kind of research…

GLORIA: Gloria.

NATHAN: Gloria. Do you get paid for this?

GLORIA: No… (*Beat.*) My husband has been gone now… 14 months and 12 days…

NATHAN: You count the days.

GLORIA: Without hesitation. It just happens.

NATHAN: It's the waiting…

GLORIA: We have to find a way of living in the waiting.

NATHAN: But if they don't come back.

GLORIA: Then your time hasn't been wasted. You should try a hobby.

NATHAN: I don't think so. I don't really have the time…

GLORIA: You have the whole of your life.

NATHAN: What if the person was your life? What if that one person was everything?

GLORIA: No one person is everything.

NATHAN: You were obviously married a long time. I don't mean to be rude. You have something to hold onto. We weren't married very long. I worry I'm forgetting her. I don't want to move on.

GLORIA: That's your choice.

NATHAN: You're very hard.

GLORIA: No.

NATHAN: Yes you are. You're hard.

GLORIA: I'm softer than I've ever been. I'm more open than I've ever been. I walk down the street and I notice people. Their pain. Their discomfort. Their happiness. I drink it in. I have my eyes open. I swim. Every day I swim. Back and forth. A routine. A boring routine that becomes so familiar I grow almost fond of it. I imagine myself swimming far out and not coming back. But how far away is forever? How far away before that place becomes my life? So I stay. In my pain, in my vulnerability, in my isolation and in this nakedness I feel reborn. Like a baby. I am standing in the world like a dripping baby. More open than I have ever been. He has made me more open than I have ever been.

NATHAN: You're not grateful? You're grateful that he left you?

GLORIA: I live with a kind of understanding.

NATHAN: Until he comes back? (*Long beat.*) What if he never comes back?

GLORIA: I live with that.

NATHAN: I thought you were meant to give people hope. I thought you were meant to show me a way to find my wife.

GLORIA: How long has she been gone…

NATHAN: Nathan.

GLORIA: Nathan.

NATHAN: 2 years, 4 months. I don't do days.

GLORIA: That's a long time. Nathan…

NATHAN: (*Long beat.*) They found her with a belt around her neck. It always throws people. She's a banker. Was a… She fucks up on some shares. I tell her she won't lose her job. She does. I tell her I love her. I tell her… She mustn't have loved me. Professional suicide. I urinate on her boss's desk a week later. Piss all over the trading room floor. It seems a riot at the time. I lose my job. With sympathy and condolences. I come home and I sit down and I realise I don't like any of the furniture. I sleep around. It makes me feel liberated. I'm envied by all my mates. The best of both worlds. A taste of both sides of the coin. Married and single. 'You lucky cunt!' I miss my wife? 'No.' (*Long beat.*) I realise that I can't remember her face yet I find her features everywhere. Fixing her eyes with the lips of others. My cleaner tells me I am sick. I get her pissed and fuck her. She doesn't speak much English but I think we don't enjoy it. She leaves. I have a new one, a man working for me now. I get myself a new job. (*Beat.*) I try to work out my wife's thoughts. Retrace her steps. She comes home. Has a sandwich. Doesn't even wash up after herself. She's lazy like that. Walks to the bathroom. Takes off her clothes, turns on the shower…

GLORIA: You're wife is dead?

NATHAN: She's missing, she's very much missing in my life.

GLORIA: (*Long beat.*) Is listening enough?

NATHAN: I don't know… I don't know if it helps at all.

GLORIA looks up from her work. NATHAN is staring out and beyond her.

The lap of water building into a shower.

Scene 21

Bar, London. TASH running in to meet HEN who sits at the bar, drinking a glass of red wine. It is raining outside. It's very quiet.

TASH: Did you not hear me? I was shouting you half way down the street. You could have an accident driving like that. I was waving my knickers off. Did you not see me? Hen…

HEN: I saw.

TASH: I thought you worked late on Thursday. If you saw me you could have given me a lift. I'm wet now. I'm really wet.

HEN: I gave in my notice.

TASH: That things on the downward slope, I should hope so. (*Looking out for barman.*) Could I?

HEN: I had to wait…

TASH: Never mind… okay… So your time is now your own.

HEN: Yeah.

TASH: That's good. That's great. This is a treat.

HEN: You always…

TASH: Use to like this bar. Do not like this bar anymore. Do not like the lack of *service*.

HEN: Don't make a fuss.

TASH: I'm not making a fuss. At least it's quiet. I thought you'd like that.

HEN: Have you been drinking?

TASH: Celebrating. The flat. It's finished, I finished the back bedroom last night. Al was well miffed.

HEN: Uh huh?

TASH: He's an arse. He's charged me a fortune.

HEN: You love me.

TASH: I love you, therefore I negotiate around him but still…

HEN: I know.

TASH: I hope you do by now because I wouldn't last another week having him in my house. He better have done me a cheap deal.

HEN: I know about you and him.

TASH: Sorry?

HEN: I know where he is on Thursday night. I know what he gets up to. (*Beat.*) I know you're sleeping with him.

TASH: Right. (*Long beat.*) And you're going to leave him?

HEN: You weren't meant to take my husband.

TASH: Partner.

HEN: Did you do this on purpose? Did you want to hurt me? Are you very unhappy, Tash? Are you so unhappy that you couldn't...? Was it so awful to see me settled? What's in you that you have to destroy everything?

TASH: That's the way you see it.

HEN: Fact.

TASH: That's the way you see it.

HEN: I don't know what to do now. What am I meant to do now? Who am I meant to go to now?

TASH: You'll make yourself...

HEN: I have this thing to shit out. I have this thing to love and look after.

TASH: Why don't we go to mine?

HEN: And I try and understand that. I try and sympathise with you. Tash, I care if you're unhappy, but it is not my fault that you can't find a man of your own. Some people find love difficult. So I've tried to be there for you and you do something like this.

TASH: He told you?

HEN: I smelt you on him.

TASH: He told you?

HEN: He came home smelling of you.

TASH: Did he say?

HEN: He's being so sweet. So nice. So desperate. Last night he cried. He said *please don't leave me.* And I realise what you do. You go in and you scorch the surface of anyone else's relationship. I'm so angry with you. I don't know what to do. I want to love you, Tash. I want to love you, but you make it hard. Perhaps you should talk to someone. You should go and see someone and talk to them, because I can't love you anymore. This baby needs me now. Al needs me now. I've tried with you. (*Beat.*) I can't trust you anymore.

TASH: But you forgive him.

HEN: No, I don't forgive him. But this is longer than a friendship. We have to be bigger than this. If you'd just come and told me how you felt, Tash. I would have understood. If you just told me you were so jealous.

TASH: He told you?

HEN: I smelt you.

TASH: He told you.

HEN: *Please don't leave me.*

TASH: She's twenty-two. The foreman's daughter. I don't know her name.

HEN: I've loved you. I've cared about you. I've shared everything with you.

TASH: He fucks her over the photocopier. They're careless with the prints.

HEN: He said you'd say this.

TASH: The girl think's she's in love with him. I found them in his bag.

HEN: Why are you doing this?

TASH: His foreman has warned Al he'll sack him if he finds him doing it again.

HEN: He said, you would…

TASH: Listen to me…I agreed he should work at mine to get him away from the site.

HEN: I promised him, I wouldn't leave him.

TASH: You can do it.

HEN: I promised him.

TASH: I didn't want to tell you.

HEN: He said…

TASH: I've never…

HEN: It's easier… (*Beat.*) Somehow it's easier if it is you…

TASH: No…

HEN: If it could have just been anybody…just anybody… then who's to say it's love with me? (*Beat.*) I smelt you on him.

TASH: No…

HEN: I smelt you on him.

TASH: Hen.

HEN: No.

TASH: My betrayal's easier than his? (*Long beat.*) There's nowhere to go then.

HEN and TASH look at one another. HEN slides over her drink. TASH knocks it back.

Scene 22

Loft, London. NATHAN is undressing as if getting ready for a shower. He drapes his shirt over the rail above. The sound of the shower throughout.

NATHAN: They fired her the day the market slumped. She never stood a chance. They're going bust. She calls me in high agitation. 'I've fucked them up the wall'. 'I'm busy, sweetheart. Can't we talk later?' (*Beat.*) Ask me how she looked that day and I struggle to remember her face. Doesn't that suck? Don't forget to look at your lover, don't forget to breath her in, taste her, know her… She took a belt… Like this one… She hooked it the shower head.

The sound of the hoover being turned off.

Why didn't the bastard break? She washed herself. Ready and then – (*Slipping the belt off around his waist.*) For a tiny moment I can feel her. Warm against my skin – (*Slipping the belt around his neck.*) I'm sorry. (*Beat.*) I get so lonely.

MARVIN enters as NATHAN swings from the rail above. MARVIN does not move for a moment until he struggles to get him down. He slips on the floor with him. He tries to revive him. He slowly realises that he is already dead.

A build of a baby's wail.

Scene 23

Flat, London. HEN packing up a tea chest of china. AL enters. He's dressed down, shorts, trainers, a younger look.

AL: I didn't see your car…

HEN: Walked.

AL: I could help you with this.

HEN: No, I'm fine… (*Beat.*) You've let this place –

AL: I was going to tidy up.

HEN: Really get a mess.

HEN goes to pick up an empty tea chest.

AL: Let me.

HEN: No.

AL: (*Long beat.*) He's sleeping?

HEN: Right through. This easy I'll have another this time next year.

AL: Your mum?

HEN: Taking me in until –

AL: The house'll –

HEN: – never be finished.

AL: – not for a while yet. I never said –

HEN: – anything that wasn't true.

AL: – sorry.

HEN: No.

AL: Sorry.

HEN: (*Long beat.*) Not accepted…

AL: Hen…

HEN: There are random moments and moments of decision. You said that…

AL: I didn't mean…

HEN: Some of the biggest moments in my life have been founded on those two principles.

AL: Hen, if I could…

HEN: No… No… Yours was a moment of decision. (*Eyeing him.*) You going on –

AL: Holiday.

HEN: Yeah.

AL: Going to India.

HEN: Yeah. (*Beat.*) With? She's young enough to be your –

AL: It's only a –

> *AL starts to help HEN pack up. They work in silence.*

What am I doing, Hen?

HEN: I don't know.

> *AL reaches out for HEN's hand. She holds it.*

AL: Please.

HEN: No. You can't come back. You can't.

Scene 24

Flat, London. Late night. TASH staggers in. She's pissed. She slams down keys and her bag and goes over to the fridge. She opens it. It casts its light, sending its hum around the room. She contemplates it.

TASH: And then what?

SQUEAL sits in the half light.

SQUEAL: There are pockets of water, just spinning in space, small oceans of water which are lifeless, dead, or as we know it at the moment but which may well have the breadth and depth of some of our own larger seas.

TASH: But what glues them together? What holds them?

SQUEAL: Gravity.

TASH: Like a skin.

SQUEAL: A skin of gravity which envelopes them and changes form in motion.

TASH: Like amoeba.

SQUEAL: Like an amoeba.

TASH: Or a puddle.

SQUEAL: Not a puddle. But they can break up.

TASH: Like a worm.

SQUEAL: I'll go with a worm. (*Beat.*) You drink too much.

TASH: I don't drink enough.

SQUEAL: I'd like to see you. I'd like to talk to you. In the daytime. Not in the dark.

TASH: You wouldn't cope.

SQUEAL: You think?

TASH holds his stare, lets this moment hang between them.

TASH: Tell me the fighter pilot story.

SQUEAL: You've heard it.

TASH: Tell me it again.

SQUEAL: I'm useless at everything, except physics. I am the maestro of physics. I do all the tests. I'm top of it all. But I can't tell the difference between green and red. Stop or go. I fail.

TASH laughs to herself, finishing off her cornflakes, laughing to herself, letting it die between them.

SQUEAL: It would be good to get further than this story you know. I'd like us to try and get beyond.

TASH: This is it.

SQUEAL: I don't believe that. I really truly don't believe that.

TASH: I wake up in the night and I'm almost breathless. Like I'm holding the exhale. Like to breath out fully will kill me, shatter me, let me feel the full breadth of my empty bed. Just me and nothing. My thoughts. And sometimes the feeling is so desperate. And the only thing that gets me to sleep is to touch myself. Run my fingers over myself, bring myself to some kind of inner connection, do something that creates an involuntary sensation, shuddering through me, like the ghost of someone, the spirit of someone fucking me. It's not that I think that people always leave. I just don't contemplate they'll stay. (*Long beat.*) It's…painful.

SQUEAL leans forward in his chair, almost touching her. TASH sits motionless, suddenly frozen, trying to focus on his face.

TASH: (*Long beat.*) I've pissed myself.

SQUEAL: Lucky I'm here then.

Scene 25

SQUEAL running, swimming towel in hand as if late for GLORIA.

SQUEAL: I'm sorry.

GLORIA: Keep your hair on. It's fine.

SQUEAL: I can't actually stay today.

GLORIA: Oh –

SQUEAL: It's just –

GLORIA: You're meeting someone? You're meeting someone.

SQUEAL: Yes.

GLORIA: Don't be miserable about it. It's good news isn't?

Silence.

I might just do a few laps.

SQUEAL: This doesn't mean –

GLORIA: What? You're dumping me? Got you worried. It's a good thing.

SQUEAL: It might just be a meeting.

GLORIA: You might be –

SQUEAL: I'm not.

GLORIA: Yeah, I'm goin to do a few laps today.

SQUEAL: Gloria –

GLORIA: Look at you. For a start, you better get your hair cut. I've been meaning to tell you for some time. Smarten up a bit for – Whoever.

SQUEAL shrugs, makes to go.

SQUEAL: From the back. The way your hair goes. The way the colour goes. First time I met you, you reminded me of my –

GLORIA: Cheeky bugger. (*Suddenly.*) I wish I had. Would have drowned you at birth. My luck.

SQUEAL: Yeah right.

GLORIA: Go on. She'll be waiting. I don't mean to be ungrateful.

SQUEAL looks away.

SQUEAL: Gloria, keep your thumbs with your fingers. It'll stop you splashing so much.

SQUEAL looks back. GLORIA has already gone, swimming away.

Scene 26

Pool, London. TASH sitting reading her book, waiting for someone
– MARVIN dressed in black. He has clearly been at a funeral. He
sits on the bench next to TASH.

MARVIN: Good book?

TASH nods. Continues reading.

Long time since I read a good book.

TASH nods. Shifts slightly in her seat. Ignores him.

Talk to me. (*Beat.*) I've just watched them bury a man.
(*Beat.*) Talk to me.

TASH: I'm sorry…

MARVIN: Say whatever you want. Say whatever comes into
your head. Just say something.

TASH: (*Long beat.*) Yes… It's a good book.

MARVIN: Adventure?

TASH: No… Sort of… A love story. Not a romantic love
story… It's a tragedy yet it also has hope. I haven't
finished it yet.

MARVIN: Of course.

TASH: Did you…

MARVIN: No. I hardly knew him.

TASH: Right. I hate funerals. It's alright if they have a lot
to drink. I've been to a wake before. You can't fail to
have a good time at a wake.

MARVIN: He was young. He was a young man.

TASH: That's awful.

MARVIN: Yes.

TASH: How did he…

MARVIN: He died because he wasn't loved, because he thought he wasn't loved.

TASH: I see. I'm sorry…

MARVIN: I come here most days.

TASH: You must be very…

MARVIN: Yes… Shaken… Yes… I'm very shaken, but I understand it you see. You think you are not loved or maybe you have stopped being able to feel that you are so you withdraw. And the hardest place to be is with people but not with people. Alone in a crowded room. And sometimes it is your fault because you don't feel anything so you have to go away in order to decide if you want to come back. And when you don't. When what you have been looking for finds you, then you hope that they will forgive you. You hope they won't feel the pain that boy felt, you hope they'll understand that you do still think of them…

TASH: I'm sure they will.

MARVIN: Becaue you have to live with the not being sure. You have to…

TASH: I'm very sorry for your loss.

MARVIN nods. TASH gets up to go.

It's a nice park. It has a view of the pool.

TASH: Yes, I guess it does.

TASH gets up to go. She leaves her book. MARVIN picks it up and starts to read it. TASH comes back for it. He hands it to her.

MARVIN: I won't be staying long anyway.

TASH takes the book, smiles and exits. MARVIN stands up. His gaze follows someone very slowly in the distance. A gentle rhythm, barely visible back and forth.

(*Silent.*) Gloria –

He turns and exits.

The lap of water.

Scene 27

Pool, London. GLORIA is standing in her swimming costume and swimming cap, dripping wet.

GLORIA: And the sea is icy but I'm not scared. I wade in quickly. It is dark and I can see the shadows of clouds moving above. The water moves around me. It's cold and yet with every stroke I feel myself getting warmer. Like being held, suspended, above it all. And soon I can't see where I have come from or how far I have gone. Just me in the water in the middle of the sea, looking up at the dark sky above. And I think how easy it would be just to let go, just to keep swimming, until I am too exhausted and my legs and arms won't hold me. I could just let the sea take me, just wash me away, when I look up and there are a pair of eyes staring back at me. A seal, staring at me, circling me. And I feel no fear, no cold just utterly and absolutely not alone. Five minutes, ten minutes no more and it's gone. And without me even doing anything I'm suddenly turning and swimming back, not looking behind me, just swimming back to the bay, swimming back to land. Just a woman, too fat for her costume, dripping wet and cold, standing on a piece of Skye. Glad she didn't drown. Glad she didn't...

GLORIA turns slowly to look behind her, as if checking for someone for a moment. Nothing. She starts to dry herself, rubbing harder as the lights go down.

The End.

Note

In addition to the above play, short snapshot scenes were added during scene changes. These are an option and are to be placed at the discretion of the production.

Insert 1

TASH runs back, hurrying after SQUEAL.

TASH: 8806 2424.

SQUEAL stops, silently amazed.

I changed my mind.

TASH turns and runs off. SQUEAL stands, silently bemused in the rain, trying to remember a telephone number.

SQUEAL: Has anyone got a pen?

Insert 2

NATHAN and MARVIN are bent perring over the fridge.

NATHAN: Fruit to the left. Dairy to the right. If you could clean it Monday, Wednesday and Friday, after you've done the surfaces and wiped through.

MARVIN: Right.

NATHAN: Hoovering thereafter.

MARVIN: Okay.

NATHAN: Good. Good.

They sit.

MARVIN: Nice fridge.

NATHAN: Thank you. I don't like my dairy and fruit too close.